The Yemens

WORLD BIBLIOGRAPHICAL SERIES

VOLUMES IN THE SERIES

1 *Yugoslavia*, John J. Horton
2 *Lebanon*, Shereen Khairallah
3 *Lesotho*, Shelagh M. Willet and David Ambrose
4 *Rhodesia/Zimbabwe*, Oliver B. Pollack and Karen Pollack
5 *Saudi Arabia*, Frank A. Clements
6 *USSR*, Anthony Thompson
7 *South Africa*, Reuben Musiker
8 *Malawi*, Robert B. Boeder
9 *Guatemala*, Woodman B. Franklin
11 *Uganda*, Robert L. Collison
12 *Malaysia*, Ian Brown and Rajeswary Ampalavanar
13 *France*, Frances Chambers
14 *Panama*, Eleanor DeSelms Langstaff
15 *Hungary*, Thomas Kabdebo
16 *USA*, Sheila R. Herstein and Naomi Robbins
17 *Greece*, Richard Clogg and Mary Jo Clogg
18 *New Zealand*, R. F. Grover
19 *Algeria*, Richard I. Lawless
21 *Belize*, Ralph Lee Woodward, Jr.
23 *Luxembourg*, Carlo Hury and Jul Christophory
24 *Swaziland*, Balam Nyeko
25 *Kenya*, Robert L. Collison
26 *India*, Brijen K. Gupta and Datta S. Kharbas
27 *Turkey*, Meral Güçlü
28 *Cyprus*, P. M. Kitromilides and M. L. Evriviades
29 *Oman*, Frank A. Clements
30 *Italy*, Emiliana P. Noether
31 *Finland*, J. E. O. Screen
32 *Poland*, Richard C. Lewański
33 *Tunisia*, Allan M. Findlay, Anne M. Findlay and Richard I. Lawless
34 *Scotland*, Eric G. Grant
35 *China*, Peter Cheng
36 *Qatar*, P. T. H. Unwin
37 *Iceland*, John J. Horton
38 *Nepal*, Dina Nath Wadhwa
39 *Haiti*, Frances Chambers
40 *Sudan*, M. W. Daly
41 *Vatican City State*, Michael J. Walsh
42 *Iraq*, Abdul Jabbar Abdulrahman
43 *United Arab Emirates*, Frank A. Clements
44 *Nicaragua*, Ralph Lee Woodward, Jr.
45 *Jamaica*, K. E. Ingram
46 *Australia*, I. Kepars
47 *Morocco*, Anne M. Findlay, Allan M. Findlay and Richard I. Lawless
48 *Mexico*, Naomi Robbins
49 *Bahrain*, P. T. H. Unwin
50 *The Yemens*, G. Rex Smith
54 *Tanzania*, Colin Darch

VOLUME 50

The Yemens

The Yemen Arab Republic and the People's Democratic Republic of Yemen

G. Rex Smith
Compiler

CLIO PRESS
OXFORD, ENGLAND · SANTA BARBARA, CALIFORNIA
DENVER, COLORADO

British Library Cataloguing in Publication Data
Smith, G. R. (Gerald Rex)
The Yemens. -- (World bibliographical series; 50)
1. Yemen – Bibliography
2. Yemen (People's Democratic Republic) – Bibliography
I. Title II. Series
016.953'3 Z3028.Y4

ISBN 0-903450-87-9

Clio Press Ltd.,
55 St. Thomas' St.,
Oxford OX1 1JG

ABC-Clio Information Services
Riviera Campus, 2040 Alameda Padre Serra,
Santa Barbara, Ca. 93103, USA

Designed by Bernard Crossland
Typeset by Berkshire Publishing Services
Printed and bound in Great Britain by
Billing and Sons Ltd., Worcester.

THE WORLD BIBLIOGRAPHICAL SERIES

This series will eventually cover every country in the world, each in a separate volume comprising annotated entries on works dealing with its history, geography, economy and politics; and with its people, their culture, customs, religion and social organization. Attention will also be paid to current living conditions – housing, education, newspapers, clothing, etc. – that are all too often ignored in standard bibliographies; and to those particular aspects relevant to individual countries. Each volume seeks to achieve, by use of careful selectivity and critical assessment of the literature, an expression of the country and an appreciation of its nature and national aspirations, to guide the reader towards an understanding of its importance. The keynote of the series is to provide, in a uniform format, an interpretation of each country that will express its culture, its place in the world, and the qualities and background that make it unique.

SERIES EDITORS

Robert L. Collison (Editor-in-chief) is Professor Emeritus, Library and Information Studies, University of California, Los Angeles, and is currently the President of the Society of Indexers. Following the war, he served as Reference Librarian for the City of Westminster and later became Librarian to the BBC. During his fifty years as a professional librarian in England and the USA, he has written more than twenty works on bibliography, librarianship, indexing and related subjects.

Sheila R. Herstein is Reference Librarian and Library Instruction Coordinator at the City College of the City University of New York. She has extensive bibliographic experience and described her innovations in the field of bibliographic instruction in 'Team teaching and bibliographic instruction', *The Bookmark*, Autumn 1979. In addition, Doctor Herstein co-authored a basic annotated bibliography in history for Funk & Wagnalls *New encyclopedia*, and for several years reviewed books for *Library Journal.*

Louis J. Reith is librarian with the Franciscan Institute, St. Bonaventure University, New York. He received his PhD from Stanford University, California, and later studied at Eberhard-Karls-Universität, Tübingen. In addition to his activities as a librarian, Dr. Reith is a specialist on 16th-century German history and the Reformation and has published many articles and papers in both German and English. He was also editor of the *American Society for Reformation Research Newsletter.*

Hans H. Wellisch is Associate Professor at the College of Library and Information Services, University of Maryland, and a member of the American Society of Indexers and the International Federation for Documentation. He is the author of numerous articles and several books on indexing and abstracting, and has also published *Indexing and abstracting: an international bibliography.* He also contributes frequently to *Journal of the American Society for Information Science, Library Quarterly,* and *The Indexer.*

To
Ḥusayn and Ḥasībah,
with great affection and gratitude

Contents

Contents

Contents

Introduction

The Yemen Arab Republic and the People's Democratic Republic of Yemen are situated in the south-west of the Arabian Peninsula. Both are Arab states and the inhabitants of the whole of the People's Democratic Republic of Yemen are Shāfi'ī Sunnī Muslims, as are those of the south and the Red Sea coastal plain of the Yemen Arab Republic, whereas those in Dhamār (see map) and the area approximately to the north belong to the Zaydiyyah, a group on the extreme liberal wing of the Shī'ah. The Yemen Arab Republic with a population of about 6,000,000 occupies roughly 75,000 square miles and the People's Democratic Republic of Yemen has a population of approximately 1,500,000 living in about 112,000 square miles. Historically both countries have formed a single area which, although never totally united in the political sense, went under the name of the Yemen. The present borders between the two were drawn up by the colonial powers, the Turks in the north, the British in the south, in the 20th century. These two countries together therefore are the subject of this bibliography.

In keeping with the aims of the series, the items listed in this selective bibliography are primarily in English and are reasonably accessible. It should, however, be stressed that, in the main for historic reasons, it has not been possible to keep solely to the English language material. The Yemen in pre-1962 (the date of the revolution) days had developed ties with Italy. Italians visited the country or took an interest in it and wrote about it. For some centuries French- and German-speakers have committed information on the country to writing. In recent years, one might say that writings in French and German have greatly multiplied in number and the trend continues. Naturally the strong colonial links between Great Britain and South Arabia, as well as the international importance of English, would in any case produce in any bibliography of the area a very large majority of items in that language. On the assumption that relatively few English-speakers can cope with Italian and German, I have excluded all but the essential items in these languages. Many English-speakers read at least some French and with French works I have felt less constraint.

The question of availability has plagued me throughout the compilation of this bibliography. Generally speaking, I have allowed the importance of an item to outweigh its relative inaccessibility. One word of caution (and perhaps of apology!) is necessary. I have long felt that, in the main through circumstances outside their control, libraries in Great Britain occasionally lack North American materials. I have at times during the compilation of this bibliography (and even before when pursuing my own work on the Yemen and in other subjects besides) stumbled across titles of North American works which appeared to me at least worthy of perusal. On further investigation, however, they have been found to be not readily available in this country. For the purposes of this bibliography, I have naturally been obliged to discard such titles.

It was the relatively kinder geographical conditions and climate of the south-west corner of the Arabian Peninsula which produced from the earliest times a settled way of life in contrast with the central and northern areas, inhabited by and large in the pre-Islamic era (i.e. pre-7th century AD) by nomadic tribes. A generous rainfall and land suitable for crop-growing brought about a developed agriculture. Since also the area lay on important trade routes, commerce flourished. Agriculture and commerce permitted the maintenance of a relatively high population level and were the mainstay of the pre-Islamic civilization of the Yemen. There was the frankincense trade too which must be specifically mentioned. Both Yemen-grown frankincense and that cultivated in Africa and passing through the area helped to sustain these civilizations which were able to levy taxes and other tolls on trade caravans traversing their territories. Though they can hardly be compared with the civilizations of ancient Egypt and Mesopotamia, the pre-Islamic South Arabian kingdoms were of considerable splendour. Their monuments and the remnants of their sophisticated irrigation systems remain in places to this day (e.g. Ma'rib/Mārib) to be admired by all, and their history and archaeology are well represented in this bibliography. I have, however, been careful to avoid the highly technical epigraphic and linguistic publications.

Scholars do not agree on precisely when these pre-Islamic kingdoms came into being. Estimates vary from the 8th century BC at the earliest to the 5th century BC. The most extensive in territory and longest in history is that of Saba, with its capital in Mārib and stretching in time from the 5th century BC to the 6th century AD. This was, without doubt, also the most important state, and most of the pre-Islamic inscriptions in the area are Sabaic. To the north, the kingdom of Maʿīn with its capital at Qarnaw, flourished in the pre-Christian era. Qatabān was centred to the east of Saba in the Bayḥān area and wielded power there at about the beginning of the Christian era. The fourth kingdom worthy of mention was that of Ḥaḍramawt with its capital at Shabwah. It was thus the most easterly of the pre-Islamic South Arabian kingdoms. All the kingdoms used a dialect form of a Semitic language extant only in the lapidary inscriptions found throughout the area. They are practical and highly formal documents in character.

It is impossible to assess accurately the process of islamization of the Yemen in the 7th and later centuries AD. One must assume that the very difficult mountainous terrain of the majority of the area would have motivated against a rapid general conversion to the new religion. We know that the Prophet Muḥammad (d. AD 632), the Orthodox (632-61), Umayyad (661-750) and Abbasid caliphs (from AD 750 onwards) all sent governors to the Yemen. These resided in Ṣanʿāʾ, al-Janad (near Taʿizz) and in Ḥaḍramawt. Certainly the Great Mosques of Ṣanʿāʾ and al-Janad were founded within the Prophet's lifetime and, although little or nothing now remains of the original buildings, they are to be reckoned as two of the earliest architectural foundations of Islam.

Again we know little of the power and influence of these early Islamic governors. It is necessary to remind the reader of the extremely difficult terrain of the Yemen. Communications must have been slow and political control over the whole area was impossible. Local petty states grew up, flourished and faded away: in AD 820-1001, the Ziyadids in Zabīd; 839-1003 the Yuʿfirids in Ṣanʿāʾ and Shibām; the Najahids, also in Zabīd, from 1012-1160; the Ismāʿīlī Shīʿī Sulayhids in Dhū Jiblah, 1047-1138, with their famous queen, Arwā bint Aḥmad; the Zurayʿids of Aden, also Ismāʿīlis, 1088-1173; the Ismāʿīlī Hamdanid sultans of Ṣanʿāʾ, 1099-1173; and the Mahdids of Zabīd, 1157-73. Thus the political map of pre-12th century Yemen was fragmented indeed.

An event of great consequence occurred in 897. A descendant of the Prophet, Yaḥyā b. Ḥusayn, arrived in the extreme north of the country from his home in Medina with a following of only some fifty persons. With great skill he promulgated his own particular Islamic message which was to be known as the Zaydiyyah. From then onwards the Zaydīs were always a force to be reckoned with in the north of the country. An imam remained at their head until 1962, the date of the republican revolution. But Zaydī doctrines live on and even today the Zaydis form the majority of the population of the Yemen Arab Republic.

An event of similarly lasting impact was the conquest in 1173 of the Yemen by a large Ayyubid army from Egypt. Tūrānshāh, the brother of the famous Saladin, occupied vast areas in the Red Sea coastal plain, Tihamah, and in the south, thus bringing them within the Ayyubid empire centred in Egypt. Even the Zaydīs in the north had to resist the advance northwards of the Ayyubid army, a mixture of Kurds, Central Asians and Persians, as well as Arabs. When their successors, the Rasulids, assumed power in 1229, the Ayyubids had successfully pacified and to a remarkable extent unified Tihāmah and the south.

The Rasulids, probably Turkoman emirs by origin, were able to build on this sound beginning and were eventually to bring about a period of political stability and great brilliance in the land (1229-1454). Their rulers too were of high quality, some distinguished writers and men of letters. They bequeathed to posterity some superb architectural monuments and where these have been published they appear below in the bibliography.

The Rasulids were followed in power in the south by a local dynasty, the Tahirids, who fell in the early 16th century to the Ottoman Turks. They took Ṣan'ā' in 1517 and were to rule over the Yemen for over a century. In 1635 the Zaydī imam, Qāsim al-Kabīr, returned the Yemen to Zaydī rule and the Turks were expelled until the late 19th century. The European powers, the British, the French and the Dutch were all engaged in trade in the Red Sea area, particularly in the Yemen in Mocha, from the 18th century onwards. This century too saw the arrival of the first European travellers. The famous Danish expedition, of which Carsten Niebuhr was the sole survivor after the deaths of all his companions from malaria, reached Hodeida in 1762. In 1872 the Ottoman Turks who had been able to re-establish a foothold on the coast of the Yemen, reoccupied the country. They remained there until after the First World War.

In 1839 the British had taken Aden and had slowly begun to deal with the rulers of the hinterland. During the years 1904-14 an Anglo-Turkish surveying team drew up the frontier between the Yemen and the British protected territory of the Aden hinterland. This frontier still today marks the boundary between the Yemen Arab Republic and the People's Democratic Republic of Yemen. In the 1950s the British developed closer relations with the rulers of the hinterland states. Advisory treaties were drawn up and a resident adviser appointed in Aden for the Western Aden Protectorate and one in al-Mukallā for the Eastern Aden Protectorate. The states of the former included the 'Abdali (centred on Lahej), the Faḍlī, the Yāfi'ī, Dathīnah, and the

Wāḥidī (previously a member of the Eastern Aden Protectorate states), while the more important states in the east were the Kathīrī and the Qu'ayṭī, both with their capitals in Wadi Ḥaḍramawt. A treaty to join in federation some of the Western Aden Protectorate states was signed in 1959, with more joining over the next few years. In 1962 arrangements were made for the crown colony of Aden to be merged into the Federation of South Arabia. The Federation collapsed in 1967 when independence from British rule was achieved in the south under the name of the People's Republic of South Yemen. This name was changed in 1970 to the People's Democratic Republic of Yemen.

On 26th September 1962 the Zaydī imam of the Ḥamīd al-Dīn family of the Yemen, Aḥmad, died and the new imam, Muḥammad al-Badr, was ousted by the revolution within a week of his taking office. He fled the country. The Yemen Arab Republic thus came into being, at first propped up only by numerous Egyptian troops who finally left the country in 1967.

Acknowledgements

It is a great pleasure to acknowledge the assistance of a number of people during the compilation of the bibliography. In Durham Miss Lesley Forbes, Keeper of Oriental Books, and her staff in the Oriental Section of the University Library are all worthy of special thanks. I should in this connection mention in particular Mrs Jill Butterworth (more of whom later) and Mr Malcolm Ferguson. In the Centre for Middle Eastern and Islamic Studies I am particularly grateful to Dr Richard Lawless, who has himself made important contributions to the World Bibliographical Series, and who gave me enormous practical help and advice. Miss Heather Bleaney gave generously of her time to help and answered my questions patiently.

In the Cambridge University Library, to which she had returned, Mrs Jill Butterworth again spared no effort to assist. I am most grateful to her. To Mr Geoffrey Roper, the compiler of the *Index Islamicus*, is also owed a debt of gratitude. My old friend Dr Robin Bidwell threw open the Middle East Centre for me and I am especially grateful to him in allowing me to browse through the materials left by the late Mr Richard Holmes. Mrs Joyce Ferguson, in her usual charming and obliging manner, rallied to my aid far beyond the call of duty.

My friend Dr Robert Wilson responded with great speed and enthusiasm to my plea for advice on maps. These entries below are in large part his own.

Finally my greatest debt must be paid to my wife, Cerries, who assumed readily the role of research assistant and saved me innumerable hours by her patient hard work.

If this bibliography assists in any way in the further understanding of the people and countries of the Yemen Arab Republic and the People's Democratic Republic of Yemen, where I have personally spent so many happy times, I shall be well content. I am proud and delighted to dedicate this book to two very special Yemenis whose company is now greatly missed. Needless to say, all the faults of this bibliography, both of omission and commission, are entirely my own.

G. Rex Smith
School of Oriental Studies
University of Durham

Theses and dissertations on The Yemens

al-T. Z. al-Abdin. 'The role of Islam in the state, Yemen Arab Republic (1940-1972)', PhD thesis, University of Cambridge, 1975.

Abdelrahman Abdalla Abdrabou. 'Relationship between reading-comprehension skills and achievement in other selected language skills of college-bound Yemeni EFL learners', PhD thesis, University of Kansas, 1983.

Nabeel Younis Abraham. 'National and local politics: a study of political conflict in the Yemeni immigrant community of Detroit, Michigan', PhD thesis, University of Michigan, 1978.

Najwa Adra. 'Qabyala: the tribal concept in the central highlands of the Yemen Arab Republic', PhD thesis, Temple University, 1982.

Ḥusayn b. 'Abdullāh al-'Amrī. 'The Yemeni scholar Muḥammad b. 'Alī al-Shawkānī (1173-1250/1760-1834) – his life, works and times, together with a critical edition of *Darr al-siḥābah fī manāqib al-qarābah wa-'l-ṣaḥābah*', University of Durham, 1983.

K. S. al-Asali. 'South Arabia in the fifth and sixth centuries C.E., with reference to relations with Central Arabia', PhD thesis, University of St. Andrews, 1967-68.

Z. R. Beydoun. 'The stratigraphy and structure of the East Aden Protectorate', DPhil thesis, University of Oxford, 1960-61.

John Richard Blackburn. 'Turkish-Yemenite political relations, 1538-68', PhD thesis, University of Toronto, 1971.

Kathryn Boals. 'Modernization and intervention: Yemen as a theoretical case study', PhD thesis, Princeton University, 1970.

A. S. Bujra. 'Social stratification of an Arab village in Ḥaḍramaut', PhD thesis, School of Oriental and African Studies, University of London, 1964-65.

Brinston Brown Collins. 'Hadramawt: crisis and intervention: 1866-81', PhD thesis, Princeton University, 1969.

J. A. Dafari. 'Ḥumainī poetry in South Arabia', PhD thesis, School of Oriental and African Studies, University of London, 1965-66.

Theses and dissertations on The Yemens

T. H. Dawood. 'The phonetics and phonology of an Aden dialect of Arabic', PhD thesis, School of Oriental and African Studies, University of London, 1951-52.

Susan Joan Dorsky. 'Women's lives in a North Yemeni highlands town', PhD thesis, Case Western Reserve University, 1981.

P. K. Dresch. 'The northern tribes of Yemen: their organisation and their place in the Yemen Arab Republic', DPhil thesis, University of Oxford, 1982.

Nabib A. Faris. 'The antiquities of South Arabia', PhD thesis, Princeton University, 1935.

Charles L. Geddes. 'The Yu'firid dynasty of Ṣan'ā'', PhD thesis, School of Oriental and African Studies, University of London, 1958-59.

L. Ghanem. 'Social aspects of the legal systems in south-west Arabia, with special reference to the application of Islamic family law in the Aden courts', MPhil thesis, School of Oriental and African Studies, University of London, 1972-73.

M. A. Ghanem. 'Verse used in San'ani songs', PhD thesis, University of London, 1968-69.

G. A. al-Gosaibi. 'The 1962 revolution in Yemen and its impact on the foreign policies of the UAR and Saudi Arabia', PhD thesis, University College, University of London, 1970-71.

A. H. F. Hamdani. 'Doctrines and history of the Isma'ili *Da'wat* in Yemen', PhD thesis, School of Oriental and African Studies, University of London, 1931.

J. G. Hartley. 'The political organisation of an Arab tribe of the Hadhramaut', London School of Economics, University of London, 1960-61.

P. G. Hill. 'The petrology of the Aden volcano, People's Democratic Republic of Yemen', PhD thesis, University of Edinburgh, 1974.

'A.-A. H. al-Hiyed. 'Relations between the Yemen and South Arabia during the Zaydī Imamate of Āl al-Qāsim, 1626-1732', PhD thesis, University of Edinburgh, 1973.

A. K. Irvine. 'A survey of old South Arabian lexical material connected with irrigation techniques', DPhil thesis, University of Oxford, 1962-63.

Saud Saadeh Jallad. 'The role of an educational technology center in the development of teacher education in the Yemen Arab Republic', PhD thesis, The Catholic University of America, 1981.

J. Ida Jiggetts. 'A study of the absorption and integration of the Yemenite Jew in the state of Israel', PhD thesis, New York University, 1957.

Theses and dissertations on The Yemens

W. I. Jones. 'The Aden dialect of Arabic: a study of its grammatical peculiarities as compared with the classical language', MA thesis, University of Wales, 1940.

Yael Katzir. 'The effects of resettlement on the status and role of Yemeni Jewish women: the case of Ramat Oranim, Israel', PhD thesis, University of California, Berkeley, 1976.

A. K. Kazi. 'A critical edition of the *Kitāb al-Muntakhab fi 'l-fiqh* of the Zaidī Imām, Yaḥyā b. al-Ḥusain, from the British Museum and Vatican MSS', PhD thesis, School of Oriental and African Studies, University of London, 1957-58.

A. O. D. Khan. 'Government accounting and internal audit in the civil service, with special reference to South Yemen', MSc thesis, University of Strathclyde, 1978.

Bar-Zion Khorman-Eraqi. 'Messianism in the Jewish community of Yemen in the nineteenth century', PhD thesis, University of California, Los Angeles, 1981.

Z. H. Kour. 'The development of Aden and British relations with neighbouring tribes, 1832-72', PhD thesis, School of Oriental and African Studies, University of London, 1975.

R. W. C. Large. 'The extension of British influence in and around the Gulf of Aden, 1865-1905', PhD thesis, School of Oriental and African Studies, University of London, 1974.

David William McClintock. 'Foreign exposure and attitudinal change: a case study of foreign policy makers in the Yemen Arab Republic', PhD thesis, University of Michigan, 1973.

A. M. A. Maktari. 'Water rights and irrigation practices in Lahj: a study of the application of customary and *Shari'ah* law in south-west Arabia', PhD thesis, University of Cambridge, 1968-69.

N. el-H. H. Mawi. 'Jews in Yemen in the 17th-19th century according to Hebrew sources with comparison with Arabic Yamani sources', PhD thesis, University of St. Andrews, 1970-71.

'Abd al-Muḥsen Medej Muḥammad al-Medej. 'Yemeni relations with the central Islamic authorities – 9-233/630-847 – a political history'. University of Durham, 1983.

Brinkley Morris Messick, III. 'Transactions in Ibb: economy and society in a Yemeni highland town', PhD thesis, Princeton University, 1978.

M. W. Mundy. 'Land and family in a Yemeni community', PhD thesis, University of Cambridge, 1982.

M. J. Norry. 'Geochemical studies of volcanics from the Karroo, Mauritius and the Aden Volcano', DPhil thesis, University of Oxford, 1977.

Theses and dissertations on The Yemens

D. J. M. Noy. 'A comparative study of magenetic surveys in the Red Sea and western Gulf of Aden', PhD thesis, University of Newcastle Upon Tyne, 1979.

S. C. Page. 'The development of Soviet policies and attitudes towards the countries of the Arabian Pensinsula', PhD thesis, University of Reading, 1970-71.

A. J. H. Reed. 'Ta'iz in the twentieth century: a study in urban development', BPhil thesis, University of Oxford, 1976.

A. M. al-Shadebi. 'A study of some tick-borne diseases of ruminant livestock in Great Britain and in the Yemen Arab Republic', MSc thesis, University of Wales, Bangor, 1978.

Uri Sharvit. 'The role of music in the Jewish Yemenite ritual: a study of ethnic persistence', PhD thesis, Columbia University, 1982.

Thomas Bruce Stevenson. 'Kinship, stratification and mobility: social change in a Yemeni highlands town', PhD thesis, Wayne State University, 1981.

Robert Wilson Stookey. 'Political change in Yemen: a study of values and legitimacy', PhD thesis, University of Texas, 1972.

P. Styles. 'Detailed magnetic surveys of the western Gulf of Aden and the southern Red Sea and their interpretation, with specific reference to the drifting apart of Arabia and Africa', PhD thesis, University of Newcastle Upon Tyne, 1977.

Jon C. Swanson. 'The consequences of emigration for economic development in the Yemen Arab Republic', PhD thesis, Wayne State University, 1978.

Roy Edward Thoman. 'Aden and South Arabia on the threshold of independence: a political analysis', PhD thesis, University of Kentucky, 1967.

B. S. Thomas. 'The geography and ethnography of unknown South Arabia', PhD thesis, University of Cambridge, 1935.

A. S. Tritton. 'The rise and progress of the Sultans of Sana'a, AD 1596-1646', DLitt thesis, University of Edinburgh, 1918.

Daniel Martin Varisco. 'The adaptive dynamics of water allocation in al-Ahjur, Yemen Arab Republic', PhD thesis, University of Pennsylvania, 1982.

Manfred Wilhelm Wenner. 'Yaman since independence: a political study, 1918-62', PhD thesis, Johns Hopkins University, 1965.

S. Western. 'An approach to the classification of arid region soils, with special reference to South Arabia', MSc thesis, University of Bristol, 1969-70.

Theses and dissertations on The Yemens

R. T. O. Wilson. 'The investigation, collection and evaluation of geographical material in Yemeni texts for the mapping of north-west Yemen', PhD thesis, University of Cambridge, 1980.

Mohammed Ahmad Zabarah. 'Traditionalism vs. modernity – internal conflicts and external penetrations: a case study of Yemen', PhD thesis, Howard University, 1976.

The Country and Its People

1 **Arabian and Islamic studies.**
Robin Bidwell, G. Rex Smith. London, New York: Longman, 1983. 282p.

A collection of articles presented to Robert Bertram Serjeant on the occasion of his retirement in 1981 from the Sir Thomas Adams's Chair of Arabic at the University of Cambridge. The articles relevant here are: 1, 'Women in Saba' (A. F. L. Beeston); 2, 'Biblical and old south Arabian institutions: some parallels' (Jacques Ryckmans); 3, 'A document concerning the sale of Ghayl al-Barmalī and al-Ghayl al-Aswad by al-Mahdī 'Abbās, imam of the Yemen' (Hussein Abdullah al-Amri); 5, 'The mosque of al-Janad' (Paolo Costa); 7, 'The apostacy of 'Alī b. al-Faḍl' (C. L. Geddes); 9, 'The painted dome of the Ashrafiyyah in Ta'izz, Yemen' (Ronald Lewcock); 13, 'Feminism and feminist movements in the Middle East, a preliminary exploration: . . . People's Democratic Republic of Yemen' (Leila Ahmed); 14, 'Some notes on the history of Socotra' (C. F. Beckingham); 16, 'Some remarks on the ritual significance of the bull in pre-Islamic south Arabia' (Walter Dostal); 17, 'Anglo-Ottoman confrontation in the Yemen: the first Mocha incident' (Caesar E. Farah); 18, 'The system of enumeration in the South Arabian languages' (T. M. Johnstone); and 20, 'Notes on some ordinances, decrees and laws of the Kathīrī sultanate' (Abdullah M. A. Maktari).

2 **Yemen.**
Bernard Gérard, translated from the French by Mostyn Mowbray. Paris: Delroisse, 1973. 140p. map. bibliog.

A lavish picture book on the Yemen Arab Republic.

3 **Pictures from Yemen.**
Richard Gerlach. Leipzig, GDR: Editions Leipzig [n.d.]. 29p. map.

A book of pictures of the Yemen taken before the 1962 revolution.

4 **Western Arabia and the Red Sea.**
Great Britain. Admiralty. Naval Intelligence Division. London: HM Stationery Office, 1946. 659p. 48 maps.

A handbook produced for official purposes during the Second World War. There is much information on South Arabia under the following headings: geology and physical geography; the coasts; climate and vegetation; history (to be read with caution!); administration; the people; public health and disease; agriculture; economic geography; and ports and towns. There are appendixes on Socotra and the Kuria Muria Islands.

5 **Research in Yemen: facilities, climate and current projects.**
Arnold H. Green, Robert W. Stookey. *Middle East Studies Association Bulletin*, vol. 8 (1974), p. 27-46.

Provides details of current research on mediaeval and modern Yemen.

6 **Al-Yemen: a general social, political and economic survey.**
Gamal-Eddine Heyworth-Dunne. Cairo: Renaissance Bookshop, 1952. 118p. map.

This book deals, for example, with: geography; history; population; government; political life; language; education; communications; economy; society; and health. Although now somewhat out-of-date, the work still provides useful information on the subjects listed above.

7 **An account of the British settlement of Aden in Arabia.**
F. M. Hunter. London: Frank Cass, 1968. 232p. 2 maps.

A new impression of a book originally published in 1877. The monograph was prepared at the request of the Government of India and includes: geography – area, population, climate, water supplies; people – races, dress, food, ceremonies, religion; supplies – grains, fodder, animals; trade – currency, industries etc.; administration – police, justice, prisons, land tenure, finance, military, education; and political relations – tribes etc. A very thorough account of 19th-century Aden.

8 **Survey of social and economic conditions in the Aden protectorate.**
Doreen Ingrams. Published by the author, printed by the Government Printer, British Administration, Eritrea, 1949. 169p. map. bibliog.

The subjects covered in this survey include: geography; population; social structure; class structure; language; religion; justice; education; health; housing; everyday life; agriculture; irrigation; industries; communications; commerce; currency; finance; and nutrition.

9 **Yémen.** (The Yemen.)
Simon Jargy. Paris: Hachette Réalités, 1978. 149p. map.

A popular book on both Yemens, full of excellent colour photographs by Alain Saint-Hilaire. The subjects examined, for example, include: pre-Islamic Yemen; the mediaeval period; the Yemen and the West; the revolution; and everyday life.

10 **City of Ṣan'ā'.**
Edited by James Kirkman. London: World of Islam Festival Trust, 1976. 83p. map. bibliog.

A catalogue of an exhibition held in the Museum of Mankind, London, for the World of Islam Festival, 1976. The market, mosques, baths, private houses, and costumes, for example, are all included in the catalogue.

11 **The Middle East: a political and economic survey.**
Edited by Peter Mansfield. Oxford, England. University Press, 1980. 5th ed. 579p. map. bibliog.

A general political and economic survey of the Middle East. Both the Yemen Arab Republic and the People's Democratic Republic of Yemen are dealt with under section 2, Arabia. The subjects examined in both cases include: agriculture; aid; banking; climate; coffee; cotton; currency; development; economy; education; emigration; exports; foreign relations; frontiers; health; history; industry; imports; irrigation; minerals; oil; politics; population; religion; transport; tribes; radio; and social conditions.

12 **Arabia Felix: the Yemen and its people.**
Pascal Maréchaux. London: Thames & Hudson, 1979. 81p. map.

An album of photographs of the Yemen Arab Republic and its inhabitants. Of the 86 illustrations, 81 are in colour. Each plate has a fairly detailed caption and there is a brief introduction.

13 **The Middle East and North Africa 1981-82.**
London: Europa Publications, 1981. 29th ed. 993p. 10 maps. bibliog.

A general reference book covering the whole area of the Middle East and North Africa. In part 3, 'Country surveys', there are sections on the Yemen Arab Republic (p. 875-91) and the People's Democratic Republic of Yemen (p. 893-914), under the headings: physical and social geography; history; economy; statistics; directory; and bibliography.

14 **Middle East Annual Review.**
Saffron Walden, England: Middle East Review Company, 1974-80. annual.

A survey of the Middle Eastern countries by individual country under such headings as: politics; economy; production; transport; and finance. Continued in 1981 by *Middle East Review* (see below).

15 **Middle East Review.**
Saffron Walden, England: World of Information, 1981- . annual.

A continuation of the *Middle East Annual Review* above.

16 **Area handbook for the Yemens.**
Richard F. Nyrop (*et al.*) Washington, DC: American University, 1977. 240p. 11 maps. bibliog. (Foreign Area Studies Series).

A handbook of the two Yemens providing a convenient compilation of the social, economic, political and military institutions and practices of both countries.

17 **Arabian Studies.**
Edited by R. B. Serjeant, R. L. Bidwell. London: C. Hurst; Totowa, New Jersey: Rowman & Littlefield (vol. 1); London: C. Hurst (vols. 2, 3 and 4); London: C. Hurst; Montreal: McGill-Queen's University Press (vol. 5); London: Scorpion Communications, for Middle East Centre, Cambridge, 1974- . annual.

This periodical covers the whole of the area of the Arabian Peninsula, but contains numerous articles on the Yemens in such fields as pre-Islamic South Arabian culture, folklore, agriculture, history, epigraphy, numismatics, archaeology, architecture and literature.

18 **Ṣan'ā': an Arabian Islamic city.**
Edited by R. B. Serjeant, Ronald Lewcock. London: World of Islam Festival Trust, 1983. 631p. 9 maps. bibliog.

A multi-contributor, profusely illustrated study of the city of Ṣan'ā'. Important contributions are as follows: pre-Islamic Ṣan'ā' (A. F. L. Beeston); early and mediaeval history (G. Rex Smith); post-mediaeval and modern history (R. B. Serjeant); urban development (Ronald Lewcock); administrative organisation (R. B. Serjeant, Ḥusayn al-'Amrī); market and business life (R. B. Serjeant); buildings of the market (Ronald Lewcock); the mint (Nicholas Lowick); the mosques (Ronald Lewcock, G. Rex Smith, R. B. Serjeant); the Jews (A. Shivtiel, Wilfrid Lockwood, R. B. Serjeant); houses (Ronald Lewcock, R. B. Serjeant); the baths (Ronald Lewcock, R. B. Serjeant); food and cookery (R. B. Serjeant, Aḥmad Qaryah, Annika Bornstein).

19 **Studies in Arabian history and civilisation.**
R. B. Serjeant. London: Variorum Reprints, 1981. 350p. map. bibliog.

A collection of some of the author's articles. The following are relevant here: 1, 'Hūd and other pre-Islamic prophets of Ḥaḍramawt'; 3, 'Ḥaram and ḥawṭah, the sacred enclave in Arabia'; 9, 'South Arabia'; 10, 'Historians and historiography of Ḥadramawt'; 11, 'Pottery and glass fragments from the Aden littoral with historical notes' (with Arthur Lane); 12, 'The ports of Aden and Shihr'; and 13, 'A journey by two Jesuits from Dhufār to Ṣan'ā' in 1590' (with C. F. Beckingham).

20 **Area handbook for the peripheral states of the Arabian Peninsula.**
Stanford Research Institute. Washington, DC: American University, 1971. 201p. 4 maps. bibliog.

A handbook of the two Yemens as well as of the Gulf states and Oman. It deals with such questions as historical background, physical environment, population, ethnic and religious groups, social structure, politics, foreign relations, economy and the military.

21 **The queen of Sheba's land: Yemen (Arabia Felix).**
Adnan Tarcici. Beirut: Nowfel, 1973. 202p. map. bibliog.

Part one has a general historical introduction. Part two deals with the Yemen Arab Republic, its industry, communications, administration, religions, social and cultural life, and geography.

22 **Le Yémen: pays de la reine de Saba.** (Yemen: land of the queen of Sheba.)
Reinhold Wepf. Bern: Kümmerly & Frey, 1967. 104p. 2 maps.

A well-illustrated popular book on the Yemen Arab Republic.

23 **Who's who in the Arab world.**
Beirut: Publitec Publications, 1981. 1,367p.

Sections 19 and 20 of part two contain entries on the Yemen Arab Republic and the People's Democratic Republic of Yemen (p. 597-623). Both sections provide information on such subjects as: geography; history; constitution; cabinet (now out of date); embassies; economy; agriculture; banking; trade; transport; medical services; education; and the press. Part 3 contains the biographical entries and includes prominent persons from both countries.

24 **Yemen Arab Republic: a special report.**
The Times (17 Nov. 1977), p. I-X.

A special *Times* report on the Yemen Arab Republic including the following subjects: labour; development; industry; agriculture; minerals; ports; ornithology; architecture; cookery; education; health; and history.

Geography

General

25 **Sand formations in Southern Arabia.**
R. A. Bagnold. *Geographical Journal,* vol. 117 (Jan.-Dec. 1951), p. 78-86.

A semi-technical study of desert sand dunes in al-Rub' al-Khālī.

26 **The Middle East: a physical, social and regional geography.**
W. B. Fisher. London: Methuen, 1971, 6th ed. 559p. maps. bibliog.

A general geography of the Middle East. The reader's attention is drawn in particular to Chapter XVIII. The Yemen is found as a heading on p. 462 and the descriptions of the two countries continue to p. 469. There is further information in parts 1 (physical) and 2 (social). See also such index entries as Aden, Hadhramaut, Sa'ana (sic) etc.

27 **Land of the Arabs.**
M. Abdel-Kader Hatem. London, New York: Longman, 1977. 323p. 31 maps. bibliog. illus.

A basic physical geography of the Arab world country by country. The Yemen Arab Republic and the People's Democratic Republic of Yemen are included on p. 299-307. The short articles on each country concentrate heavily on the climate and agriculture and include photographs, maps and a diagram illustrating land use. There is a short bibliography on p. 305 covering both countries.

Al-Yemen: a general social, political and economic survey.
See item no. 6.

An account of the British settlement of Aden in Arabia.
See item no. 7.

Survey of social and economic conditions in the Aden protectorate.
See item no. 8.

Arabian Studies.
See item no. 17.

Ṣan'ā': an Arabian Islamic city.
See item no. 18.

The queen of Sheba's land: Yemen (Arabia Felix).
See item no. 21.

Le Yémen: pays de la reine de Saba. (Yemen: land of the queen of Sheba).
See item no. 22.

Who's who in the Arab world.
See item no. 23.

Yémen. (The Yemen).
See item no. 43.

Democratic Yemen today.
See item no. 44.

Lahdj.
See item no. 134.

The antiquities of South Arabia.
See item no. 146.

'Adan.
See item no. 168.

The Ayyubids and early Rasulids in the Yemen.
See item no. 176.

Ḥaḍramawt.
See item no. 178.

Das Qāt. (Qat).
See item no. 261.

Emigration and economic development: the case of the Yemen Arab Republic.
See item no. 331.

Asia.
See item no. 340.

Theses on Islam, the Middle East and North-west Africa 1880-1978.
See item no. 400.

The Near East (South-west Asia and North Africa): a bibliographic study.
See item no. 401.

Special features

28 **Seismicity of Yemen.**
N. N. Ambraseys, C. P. Melville. *Nature*, vol. 303, no. 5915 (May 1983), p. 321-23.

After the 1982 earthquake centred in the Yemen Arab Republic, the authors, a seismologist and an Arabist, investigate the history of earthquakes in the area. Their main conclusion is that the seismicity of the Peninsula is, contrary to common belief, high.

Western Arabia and the Red Sea.
See item no. 4.

An account of the British settlement of Aden in Arabia.
See item no. 7.

The Middle East: a political and economic survey.
See item no. 11.

Democratic Yemen today.
See item no. 44.

Socotra: 'Island of Bliss'.
See item no. 58.

Arabia infelix or the Turks in Yemen.
See item no. 59.

The land of Uz.
See item no. 78.

Emigration and economic development: the case of the Yemen Arab Republic.
See item no. 331.

Yemen Arab Republic.
See item no. 346.

Geology

29 **Geology of the Arabian Peninsula: Eastern Aden Protectorate and part of Dhufar.**
Z. R. Beydoun. Washington, DC: US Government Printing Office, 1966. 49p. bibliog.

A review of the geology of the Eastern Aden Protectorate and part of Dhofar as shown on United States Geological Survey Miscellaneous Geologic Investigation Map I – 270A, 'Geologic map of the Arabian Peninsula', 1963.

Western Arabia and the Red Sea.
See item no. 4.

Democratic Yemen today.
See item no. 44.

Socotra: 'Island of Bliss'.
See item no. 58.

Yemen Arab Republic.
See item no. 346.

Theses on Islam, the Middle East and North-west Africa 1880-1978.
See item no. 400.

Maps

30 **An air reconnaissance of the Hadhramaut.**
R. A. Cockrane. *Geographical Journal*, vol. 77, no. 3 (March 1931), p. 209-16.

Examines air reconnaissance and mapping in the Ḥaḍramawt.

31 **People's Democratic Republic of Yemen: official standard names gazetteer.**
Prepared by the Defense Mapping Agency Topographic Center. Washington, DC: US Board on Geographic Names, 1976. 204p. map.

An alphabetical list of the official standard names of the country approved by the Board.

32 **Yemen Arab Republic: official standard names gazetteer.**
Prepared by the Defense Mapping Agency Topographic Center. Washington, DC: US Board on Geographic Names, 1976. 124p. map.

An alphabetical list of the official standard names of the country approved by the Board.

33 **Administrative division and land use in the Yemen Arab Republic.**
U. Geiser, H. Staffen. Bern, Ṣan'ā', 1977. Scale: 1:500,000. 1 sheet.

A photographic reduction of a map from the British Ministry of Defence *Yemen Arab Republic* maps (see below), with graticule and contour lines, but without grid and layer tints. Additional detail includes: corrections to place-names and some additional place-names; province and district boundaries with names in English and Arabic; land use indicated with stippled tints.

34 **Population distribution, administrative division and land use in the Yemen Arab Republic.**
U. Geiser, H. Staffen. Bern, Ṣan'ā', 1977. Scale: 1:500,000. 1 sheet.

See the above entry for contents description. Provides additional information on population distribution.

35 **The Yemen Arab Republic and surrounding areas.**
London: Great Britain. Ministry of Defence. HM Stationery Office, 1974. Scale: 1:250,000. 8 sheets.

A series of maps produced by the British government to assist in the planning of projects in the Yemen Arab Republic. The maps are provided with graticule (15′ intervals) and Universal Transverse Mercator grid (10km squares). Topography is shown by contours at 100m intervals (with some 50m supplementary lines) and layer tints.

36 **Yemen Arab Republic: YAR 500 (K465).**
Great Britain. Ministry of Overseas Development. HM Stationery Office, 1978. Scale: 1:500,000. 1 sheet.

This is a map reproduced from the Ministry of Defence *Yemen Arab Republic* (see above) showing only general topography with contour lines and layer tints at 500m intervals (with supplementary contour tint at 250m above sea level). The naming has been provided from ground surveys and additional sources. The map shows relative settlement size and importance, district names, routes and additional detail. Includes Universal Transverse Mercator grid (10km squares), with graticule intersections at 30′ intervals.

37 **Yemen Arab Republic: YAR 50.**
Great Britain. Ministry of Overseas Development. London: HM Stationery Office, 1979- . Scale: 1:500,000.

A series which is still in production, produced for the Survey Department, Ministry of Public Works, Ṣan'ā'. This detailed series of maps was produced as a result of aerial photography and detailed ground surveys of districts accessible by motor car. The sheets cover an area approximately 27km by 27km square (15′ by 15′). Universal Transverse Mercator grid is shown at 1000m intervals, gradicule indicated at sheet edges.

38 **Atlas of Islamic history.**
Compiled by Harry W. Hazard, maps executed by H. Lester Cooke, J. McA. Smiley. Princeton, New Jersey: Princeton University Press, 1951. 43p. 20 maps. (Princeton Oriental Studies, no. 12).

An atlas of general reference maps for use by students, businessmen and government officials concerned with Middle East affairs. The work illustrates, in particular, the spread of Islam throughout the area. It provides maps showing the boundaries of the territories ruled by the Yemeni dynasties and provides a short historical summary of the events of each century.

39 **The maps of Carsten Niebuhr 200 years after.**
I. W. J. Hopkins. *Cartographic Journal*, vol. 4, no. 1 (June 1967), p. 115-18.

An assessment of the maps produced by Carsten Niebuhr. See Niebuhr's *Travels through Arabia . . .* (q.v.) for his own account.

40 **A contribution to the geography and cartography of north-west Yemen.**
Josef Werdecker. *Bulletin de la Société royale de Géographie d'Egypte*, vol. 20 (1939), p. 1-160.

An extremely important article of some length on various aspects of the geography of north-west Yemen. The author's study is based on the recorded exploration of the area by Eduard Glaser in the years 1882-84. There is a biography of Glaser, an account of his expeditions, a gazetteer of place-names, a bibliography, index and two maps.

41 **A new map of Southern Arabia.**
Hermann von Wissman. *Geographical Journal*, vol. 124 (1958), p. 163-67.

An introduction to Wissman's map of *Southern Arabia* (see below). Part 1 is entitled 'Basis and compilation of the map'. Part 2 of this article is entitled 'Problem of place names' and was written by R. B. Serjeant.

42 **Southern Arabia.**
Compiled by H. von Wissmann, rendering and partial correction of the place-names prepared by R. B. Serjeant. London: Royal Geographical Society, 1958. Scale: 1.500,000. 2 sheets.

This map covers the area from Shuqrā and Bayḥān in the west to al-Shiḥr and Ḥaḍramawt in the east. Mountains, formlines, heights, passes, water courses, wells, and areas of cultivation, sand, and volcanoes are all indicated.

A contribution to the population geography of the Yemen Arab Republic.
See item no. 227.

Yemen Arab Republic.
See item no. 346.

Tourism

43 **Yémen.** (The Yemen.)
Claudie Fayein. Paris: Seuil, 1975. 188p. bibliog. illus. (Collections Microcosme Petite Planète, no. 49).

A guidebook to the Yemen Arab Republic and the People's Democratic Republic of Yemen. This volume is part of a world series, organized on a country by country basis. Aimed at the tourist the book is illustrated and covers such subjects as history, geography, economy, health, education, the press, and justice.

44 **Democratic Yemen today.**
Farouk M. Luqman. Printed in Bombay, 1970. 206p. map.

A popular guide to the People's Democratic Republic of Yemen. The chapters include: geography and climate; history; economy; agriculture; the port of Aden; government; development; geology; archaeology; and flora and fauna.

45 **Yemen 1970.**
Farouk M. Luqman. Aden, 1970. 150p.

A popular guide to the Yemen Arab Republic.

46 **Tourism in Democratic Yemen.**
Photography by Xavier Richer. Paris: Editions Delcroisse, 1976. 228p. illus.

A tourist guide to the People's Democratic Republic of Yemen in English, French, German and Arabic. The volume is lavishly illustrated.

Le Yémen: pays de la reine de Saba. (Yemen: land of the queen of Sheba).
See item no. 22.

Travellers' Accounts

47 **Inquiétant Yémen.** (The disturbing Yemen.)
François Balsan. Paris, Geneva: La Palatine, 1961. 234p. illus.

A journalistic description of a journey to the Yemen, with attempts to analyse the social and economic life of the country in the late 1950s. The work includes black and white photographs.

48 **Dutch travellers in Arabia in the seventeenth century. Parts I and II.**
Charles F. Beckingham. *Journal of the Royal Asiatic Society*, (April 1951), p. 64-81; and (Oct. 1951), p. 170-81.

An account of various Dutch expeditions to Arabia, including South Arabia.

49 **A journey by two Jesuits from Dhufar to Ṣan'ā' in 1590.**
C. F. Beckingham, R. B. Serjeant. *Geographical Journal*, vol. 115 (Jan.-June 1950), p. 194-207.

Describes the journey made by two Jesuits to Ṣan'ā', with an illustration and map.

50 **Some early travels in Arabia.**
Charles F. Beckingham. *Journal of the Royal Asiatic Society* (Oct. 1949), p. 155-76.

An account written by some early travellers in the Arabian Peninsula, including South Arabia.

51 **The kingdom of Melchior: adventure in south west Arabia.**
The Master of Belhaven. London: John Murray, 1949. 212p. 2 maps.

The reminiscences of a British officer in the Aden Protectorate of the 1930s which includes much information on the social conditions and tribal organization of the area. There is also an account of the author's mission to the Yemeni authorities in Ṣan'ā' and a brief appendix, with musical scores, of local songs and chants.

Travellers' Accounts

52 **The uneven road.**
Lord Belhaven. London: John Murray, 1955. 335p. 2 maps.

An autobiography, much of it concerning the author's days as a British officer in the Aden Protectorate. Parts 2, 3 and 4 are of direct interest and recount in some detail the author's work in Quṭaybī, Faḍlī and Ṣubayḥī territories.

53 **Southern Arabia.**
Theodore Bent (and Mrs Theodore Bent). London: Smith, Elder, 1900. 455p. 3 maps. bibliog.

The authors recall their 19th-century travels in Ḥaḍramawt, Socotra, Faḍlī and Yāfi'ī territory. Oman, Dhofar and the eastern Sudan are also included.

54 **Yemen on the threshold.**
Erich W. Bethmann. Washington, DC: American Friends of the Middle East, 1960. 78p. map. illus.

An account of a journey in 1959 in the Yemen, in particular in the Ta'izz, Ṣan'ā', Ibb, Yarīm, Dhamār and Mārib areas. The coloured photographs are few in number and of poor quality.

55 **Travellers in Arabia.**
Robin Bidwell. London, New York, Sydney, Toronto: Hamlyn, 1976. 224p. 2 maps. bibliog.

An illustrated study of the more famous European travellers in the Arabian Peninsula. Carsten Niebuhr's expedition (*Travels through Arabia,* q.v.) occupies a whole chapter (p. 32-50) and another chapter is entitled 'Travellers in south-west Arabia' (p. 162-92).

56 **Island of the dragon's blood.**
Douglas Botting. London: Hodder & Stoughton, 1958. 251p. 2 maps. bibliog.

A rare general account of the island of Socotra and its people.

57 **The Oxford University expedition to Socotra.**
Douglas Botting. *Geographical Journal*, vol. 124, no. 2 (June 1958), p. 200-09.

A description of the 1956 expedition which includes archaeological, anthropological and biological notes. There are photographs and a map.

58 **Socotra: 'Island of Bliss'.**
P. C. Boxhall. *Geographical Journal*, vol. 132, part 2 (June 1966), p. 213-25.

The report of the British Army expedition to Socotra, December 1964-February 1965. Maps are provided, together with a bibliography and there are notes on climate, geology, agriculture, fishing and the life of the inhabitants.

59 **Arabia infelix or the Turks in Yamen.**
G. Wyman Bury. London: Macmillan, 1915. 208p. 3 maps.

A report of a journey through Turkish-occupied Yemen. The chapter headings include: 4, 'Sanaa'; 5, 'Birds and beasts'; 6, 'Crops and climate'; and 7, 'Trade and traders'.

60 **Yémen 62-69: de la révolution 'sauvage' à la trève des guerriers.**
(The Yemen 62-69: from the 'savage' revolution to the warriors' truce.)
Claude Deffarge, Gorian Troeller. Paris: Robert Laffont, 1969. 303p. map.

An account by two French journalists of the 1962 revolution in the Yemen and the years which followed. Appendixes include a portrait of Imam Aḥmad and a description of the Jews in the Yemen.

61 **A French doctor in the Yemen.**
Claudie Fayein, translated from the French by Douglas McKee. London: Robert Hale, 1957. 273p.

The personal reminiscences of a woman doctor in the Yemen in the 1950s.

62 **A French family in the Yemen.**
Louise Février. *Arabian Studies*, vol. 3 (1976), p. 127-35.

The personal account of the stay of a French doctor's wife in the Yemen during the period 1947-48. After her husband's death she was detained in the Yemen as a result of the assassination of Imam Yaḥyā and the failed *coup d'état*. Some of those events she describes vividly in this article.

63 **A visit to the Idrisi territory in 'Asir and Yemen.**
Rosita Forbes (Mrs. McGrath). *Geographical Journal*, vol. 62 (July-Dec. 1923), p. 271-78.

A description of a journey in north-western Yemen and 'Asīr in 1922, with photographs and map.

64 **Explorers of Arabia from the Renaissance to the Victorian era.**
Zahra Freeth, H. U. F. Winstone. London: Allen & Unwin, 1978. 308p. 9 maps. bibliog.

Contains accounts of nine expeditions by Europeans in Arabia. Chapter 3 is entitled 'Carsten Niebuhr: the lone survivor'.

Travellers' Accounts

65 **Travels in Yemen.**

Hayyim Habshush, edited by S. D. Goitein. Jerusalem: Hebrew University Press, 1941. 102p. (English text).

An account of Joseph Halévy's journey to Najrān in 1870 as told by his Jewish Ṣan'ānī guide. The editor provides a detailed summary in English and a glossary of Ṣan'ānī words. The chapters include: 1, 'How Habshush became Halévy's companion' (p. 15-18); 2, 'Habshush's adventures in Ghaiman' (p. 18-21); 3, 'Halévy visits the Muslim quarters of San'a' (p. 21-24); 4, 'Departure from San'a. Journey to Nihm' (p. 24-29); 5, 'The country of Nihm' (p. 29-43); 6, 'The journey to the Jauf' (p. 43-54); 8, 'The journey to Najran' (p. 55-58); 'From the Jauf to Marib' (p. 65-67); and 12, 'Marib and the return to San'a' (p. 67-72); There are also notes on the language of the text and a glossary of vernacular words.

66 **Arabia Felix: the Danish expedition of 1761-67.**

Thorkild Hansen, translated from the Danish by James McFarlane, Kathleen McFarlane. London: Collins, 1964. 381p. map. bibliog.

A slightly abridged translation of *Det Lykkelige Arabien,* the fascinating account of Carsten Niebuhr's expedition to Egypt and the Yemen on which Niebuhr was the only member of the party to survive. The account of the expedition's trials in the Yemen begins on p. 212 with the landing at al-Luḥayyah. The expedition travelled down through Tihāmah, passing through Bayt al-Faqīh and on to Ta'izz, Dhū Jiblah, Yarīm and other towns in the South of the Yemen were also visited by the ill-fated party. See also the entries for *Travellers in Arabia, Explorers of Arabia,* and *Travels through Arabia* for Niebuhr's story.

67 **A journey through the Yemen and some general remarks upon that country.**

Walter B. Harris. Edinburgh, London: Blackwood, 1893. 372p. map. illus.

Describes a 19th-century journey in the Yemen and includes illustrations and drawings by the author.

68 **The first crossing of southwestern Arabia.**

Hans Helfritz. *Geographical Review*, vol. 25, no. 3 (1935), p. 395-407.

An account of a journey in 1933 from al-Mukallā to Hodeida, via Ḥaḍramawt, Shabwah, Bayḥān and Ṣan'ā'.

69 **The Yemen: a secret journey.**

Hans Helfritz, translated from the German by M. Heron. London: George Allen & Unwin, 1958. 180p. map.

A somewhat exaggerated popular account of the author's visit to the Yemen via Bayḥān in the then Western Protectorate. Among other items the author describes an audience with Imam Yaḥyā.

70 **Excursion into the Hajr province of Hadramaut.**
Doreen Ingrams. *Geographical Journal*, vol. 98, no. 3. (Sept. 1941), p. 121-34.

Discusses a journey to the Western region of the Ḥaḍramawt.

71 **From Cana (Husn Ghorab) to Sabbatha (Shabwa): the South Arabian incense road.**
Harold Ingrams. *Journal of the Royal Asiatic Society* (Oct. 1945), p. 169-85.

An account of a journey following the ancient incense route.

72 **The exploration of tne Aden Protectorate.**
W. H. Ingrams. *Geographical Review*, vol. 28, no. 4 (Oct. 1938), p. 638-51.

A historical survey of exploration in South Arabia.

73 **Perfumes of Araby: silhouettes of al-Yemen.**
Harold Jacob. London: Martin Secker, 1915. 255p.

The personal reminscences of a British official in South Arabia in the early 20th century.

74 **Arabica.**
Comte de Landberg. Leiden, the Netherlands: Brill, 1898. vol. 5. 251p.

A geographical consideration of the Bayḥān, Wāḥidī, Jirdān and Shabwah areas of South Arabia and the Yemen.

75 **The barren rocks of Aden.**
James Lunt. London: Herbert Jenkins, 1966. 182p. 6 maps. bibliog.

A personal account of the author's time spent as an officer in the Arab Legion and as Commander of the Army of the Federation of South Arabia.

76 **The war in the Yemen.**
Neil McLean. *Royal Central Asian Journal*, vol. 51, no. 1 (Jan. 1964), p. 102-11.

An address to the Royal Central Asian Society (now the Royal Society for Asian Affairs) giving a personal account of the civil war in the Yemen as seen from the Royalist side.

77 **William Leveson Gower in the Yemen, 1903.**
Eric Macro. *Arabian Studies*, vol. 5 (1979), p. 141-47.

A consideration of a British naval officer's own report of his journey to the Yemen.

78 **The land of Uz.**
Abdullah Mansur (G. Wyman Bury). London: Macmillan, 1911. 354p. map.

A description of Southern Arabia in the early 20th century. The author deals firstly with those tribes within the Aden Protectorate; then more far-flung districts which had no relations with the British in the area, including the 'Awlaqīs, Bayḥān and Dathīnah. The climate, agriculture and botany of the country are also briefly mentioned.

79 **El Yemen: tre anni nell' Arabia Felice.** (Yemen: three years in Arabia Felix.)
Renzo Manzoni. Rome: Tipografia Eredi Botta, 1884. 446p. 2 maps.

An account of journeys through Turkish-occupied Yemen from Aden to Ṣan'ā'. The author touches on many aspects of life at that time.

80 **Aden to the Hadramaut: a journey in South Arabia.**
D. van der Meulen. London: John Murray, 1947. 254p. map.

An account of the author's extensive travels in Southern Arabia in the 1930s.

81 **Hadramaut: some of its mysteries unveiled.**
D. van der Meulen, H. von Wissmann. Leiden, the Netherlands: E. J. Brill, 1932. 2 maps.

An account of an expedition through Wadi Ḥaḍramawt in the early 20th century.

82 **Into burning Hadhramaut.**
D. van der Meulen. *National Geographic Magazine*, vol. 62, no. 4 (Oct. 1932), p. 387-429.

A lavishly illustrated description of Ḥaḍramawt in the 1920s and 1930s.

83 **Travels through Arabia and other countries in the East.**
Carsten Niebuhr, translated from the German by Robert Heron. Beirut: Librairie du Liban [ca. 1970]. reprint. 2 vols. (Rare Books Reprints, no. 1/I).

This is Niebuhr's own account, first published in English in Edinburgh in 1792, of the ill-fated Danish Expedition to Arabia. Volume 1 contains material on Egypt and the Red Sea journey south. The material on Yemen begins with section 8, p. 246. Volume 2 contains section 15, 'Of Yemen in general'; 19, 'Of the dominions of the Imam of Sana'; and 20, 'Of the province of Hadramaut'. This work provides remarkable insights into several aspects of the Yemen, including, for example, everyday life, administration and flora and fauna.

84 **Halévy in Yemen.**
H. St. J. B. Philby. *Geographical Journal*, vol. 102 (July-Dec. 1943), p. 116-24.

A study of Joseph Halévy's journey through the Jawf region of Yemen, collating the version of Habshush (*Travels in the Yemen*, q.v.) with Halévy's account.

85 **Sheba's daughters: being a record of travel in Southern Arabia.**
H. St. J. B. Philby. London: Methuen, 1939. 485p. map.

An illustrated travel account including an appendix 'On the inscriptions discovered by Mr. Philby' by A. F. L. Beeston. The inscriptions in question are pre-Islamic Epigraphic South Arabian.

86 **Land and peoples of the Hadhramaut, Aden protectorate.**
Ruthven W. Pike. *Geographical Review* (New York), vol. 30, no. 4 (Oct. 1940), p. 627-48.

A description of the Ḥaḍramawt and its people in the 1930s.

87 **Arabian peak and desert: travels in al-Yaman.**
Ameen Rihani. London: Constable, 1930. 280p.

A Syrian's view of the Yemen of the 1920s.

88 **San'a past and present.**
William Robertson. *Moslem World*, vol. 33, no. 1 (Jan. 1943), p. 52-57.

The author provides brief notes on the city of Ṣan'ā'.

89 **In the high Yemen.**
Hugh Scott. New York: AMS Press, 1975. reprint. 260p. 4 maps. bibliog.

The account by a naturalist of his journey in the late 1930s from Aden into the Yemen to Ṣan'ā' and from Ṣan'ā' to Hodeida on the Red Sea coast. The author includes an introduction on the natural history of the Yemen and ends with a historical section, the Yemen from early times and prospects for the future.

90 **A journey to the Yemen.**
Hugh Scott. *Geographical Journal*, vol. 93, no. 2 (Feb. 1939), p. 97-125.

An account of a naturalist's visit to the Yemen. See also the above entry.

Travellers' Accounts

91 **The Yemen in 1937-38.**
Hugh Scott. *Journal of the Royal Central Asian Society,* vol. 27 (Jan. 1940), p. 21-44.

Comments on the historical, sociological and political conditions in the Yemen of the period.

92 **Notes on Ṣubaiḥī territory, West of Aden.**
R. B. Serjeant. *Le Muséon*, vol. 66. (1953), p. 123-31.

Provides geographical and historical notes on the Ṣubayḥī territory.

93 **Arabian assignment.**
David Smiley, with Peter Kemp. London: Leo Cooper, 1975. 239p. 2 maps.

A British army officer's personal assessment of the civil war in the Yemen after the 1962 revolution. Part 2 concerns the Yemen and deals in some detail with the tactics of the Royalists in the civil war and what the author considers to be their mistakes.

94 **Tribes and tribulations: a journey in republican Yemen.**
Peter Somerville-Large. London: Robert Hale, 1967. 187p. map.

A journalist's description of the Yemen Arab Republic shortly after the 1962 revolution.

95 **East is west.**
Freya Stark. London: John Murray, 1947. reprint. 218p.

The author's personal experiences of the Middle East during the Second World War. Part 1 is devoted to South Arabia.

96 **An exploration in the Hadramaut and journey to the coast.**
Freya Stark. *Geographical Journal*, vol. 93, no. 1 (Jan. 1939), p. 1-17.

A report of a journey in Haḍramawt and down to the Indian Ocean coast.

97 **In southwestern Arabia in wartime.**
Freya Stark. *Geographical Review* (New York), vol. 34, no. 3 (July 1944), p. 349-64.

The author recounts her journeys in Southern Arabia during the Second World War.

98 **Seen in the Hadhramaut.**
Freya Stark. London: John Murray, 1938. 199p.

An album of historic photographs taken in the Ḥaḍramawt of the 1930s.

99 **Some pre-Islamic inscriptions on the frankincense route in Southern Arabia.**
Freya Stark. *Journal of the Royal Asiastic Society* (July 1939), p. 479-98.

A description of the frankincense route of South Arabia and some of the pre-Islamic inscriptions found there by the author.

100 **The southern gates of Arabia.**
Freya Stark. London: John Murray, 1936. 317p. 2 maps. bibliog.

An illustrated description of a journey in Ḥaḍramawt.

101 **A winter in Arabia.**
Freya Stark. London: John Murray. Reprinted, 1945. 260p. 2 maps.

The author recalls a journey she made in the 1930s into Wadi Ḥaḍramawt.

102 **A new journey in southern Arabia.**
Wilfred Thesiger. *Geographical Journal*, vol. 108, nos. 4-6 (Oct.-Dec. 1946), p. 129-45.

The author considers a journey he made in the 1940s from Oman to Wadi Ḥaḍramawt.

103 **A modern pilgrim in Mecca and a siege in Sanaa.**
A. J. B. Wavell. London: Constable, 1918. 232p. map.

Describes a journey to Mecca and travel experiences in the Yemen. Chapter 13 contains an account of the siege of Turkish-held Ṣan'ā' in 1911.

104 **Travels in Arabia.**
J. R. Wellsted. London: John Murray, 1838. 2 vols. 4 maps.

The 19th-century travel accounts of a British naval officer lieutenant. Volume 1 concerns Oman and the pre-Islamic South Arabian site of Naqab al-Ḥajar (p. 405). Volume 2 covers, for example, Sinai, Aqabah, the Red Sea coasts, Aden (p. 382), Lahej (p. 405), Ḥuṣn al-Ghurāb (p. 421), al-Mukallā (p. 427), Ḥaḍramawt (p. 440), and al-Shiḥr (p. 443). Wellsted was greatly interested in the antiquities of the area, but was also a keen observer of the people and their customs.

A contribution to the geography and cartography of north-west Yemen.
See item no. 40.

An archaeological journey to Yemen.
See item no. 119.

Archaeological sites in the Western Aden Protectorate.
See item no. 120.

Travellers' Accounts

The Periplus of the Erythraean Sea.
See item no. 148.

Arab navigation in the Indian Ocean before the coming of the Portuguese.
See item no. 181.

Arabia in the fifteenth century navigational texts.
See item no. 182.

The first days of British Aden: the diary of John Studdy Leigh.
See item no. 207.

A select bibliography of Yemen Arab Republic and People's Democratic Republic of Yemen.
See item no. 393.

Flora and Fauna

105 **The natural history of Sokotra and Abd-el-Kuri.**
Edited by Henry O. Forbes. Liverpool, England: Museums Committee, 1903. 598p. map. illus.

A scientific study of the natural history of the island of Socotra which contains the work of a number of different contributors. The volume covers mammals, birds, reptiles, insects and plants. There are numerous illustrations, some in colour.

106 **The mammals of Arabia.**
David L. Harrison. London: Ernest Benn, 1964-72. 3 vols. map. bibliog.

The work deals with mammals in the wider context of the Middle East, despite the title. Full zoological descriptions are given and the work is of great value as a reference book. Distribution maps occur with each species, enabling the user to see at a glance mammals found in Southern Arabia.

107 **Arabian and African frankincense trees.**
F. Nigel Hepper. *Journal of Egyptian Archaeology,* vol. 55 (1969), p. 66-72.

A botanical study of the frankincense of the Dhofar and eastern Ḥaḍramawt regions.

108 **Porcupines in the Yemen.**
R. B. Serjeant. *Arabian Studies*, vol. 1 (1974), p. 180.

Provides brief notes on the occurrence of the porcupine (*Hystrix indica*) in the Yemen.

Yemen Arab Republic: a special report.
See item no. 24.

Democratic Yemen today.
See item no. 44.

The Oxford University expedition to Socotra.
See item no. 57.

Flora and Fauna

Arabia infelix or the Turks in Yamen.
See item no. 59.

The land of Uz.
See item no. 78.

Travels through Arabia and other countries in the East.
See item no. 83.

In the high Yemen.
See item no. 89.

A journey to the Yemen.
See item no. 90.

Arabian frankincense in antiquity according to classical sources.
See item no. 151.

Das Qāt. (Qat).
See item no. 261.

South Arabian hunt.
See item no. 265.

The possible origin of the dwarf cattle of Socotra.
See item no. 344.

Yemen Arab Republic.
See item no. 346.

The cultivation of cereals in medieval Yemen.
See item no. 347.

Guarding crops against *am-sibrītah* in north-west Yemen.
See item no. 350.

Folklore and folk literature in Oman and Socotra.
See item no. 377.

Folk-remedies from Ḥaḍramawt.
See item no. 378.

Prehistory and Archaeology

109 **Archaeological discoveries in south Arabia.**
Richard LeBaron Bowen, Frank P. Albright. Baltimore, Maryland: Johns Hopkins Press, 1958. 315p. 8 maps. bibliog. (Publications of the American Foundation for the Study of Man, Report of the American Foundation, no. 2).

The report of the American Foundation expeditions to the Yemen in the period 1950-52. The contents include: 'Archaeological survey of Beiḥân (Bayḥān)'; 'Ancient trade routes'; 'Irrigation in ancient Qataban'; 'Burial monuments of South Arabia'; 'Ancient frankincense-producing areas'; and 'Excavations at Mârib'.

110 **The tombs and Moon Temple of Hureidha (Hadhramaut).**
G. Caton Thompson. London: Society of Antiquaries, 1944. 184p. bibliog. illus. (Reports of the Research Committee of the Society of Antiquaries of London, no. 13).

A study of the pre-Islamic antiquities of Ḥuraydah, Ḥadramawt. The book contains numerous plates, line drawings and diagrams.

111 **An ancient south Arabian necropolis: objects from the second campaign (1951) in the Timna' cemetery.**
Ray L. Cleveland. Baltimore, Maryland: Johns Hopkins Press, 1965. 188p. illus. (Publications of the American Foundation for the Study of Man, no. 4).

An archaelogical report on Timna', the pre-Islamic site in Bayḥān.

112 **The pre-Islamic antiquities at the Yemen National Museum.**
Paolo M. Costa. Rome: 'L'Erma' di Bretschneider, 1978. 52p. map. illus. (Studia Archaeologica, no. 19).

A guide to the pre-Islamic antiquities on display in the Yemen National Museum in Ṣan'ā'. The work includes numerous photographs of the exhibits.

Prehistory and Archaeology

113 **Archäologische Berichte aus dem Jemen.** (Archaeological reports from the Yemen.)

Deutsches Archäologisches Institut Ṣan'ā'. Mainz am Rhein, GFR: Verlag Philipp von Zabern, 1982. 278p. 2 maps.

This first volume of a series contains a detailed archaeological and epigraphic study of pre-Islamic Mārib. The work also covers some Islamic monuments including the Great Mosque of Ṣan'ā' and the mosque of Dhū Jiblah.

114 **Ancient capitals from Aden.**

Brian Doe. *Arabian Studies*, vol. 1 (1974), p. 176-79.

Provides brief notes on two ancient 'classical' capitals discovered in Crater, Aden.

115 **Ḥuṣn al-Ġurāb and the site of Qana'.**

Brian Doe. *Le Muséon*, vol. 74 (1961), p. 191-98.

A description of the pre-Islamic sites of Ḥuṣn al-Ghurāb and Qana'.

116 **Pottery sites near Aden.**

D. Brian Doe. *Journal of the Royal Asiatic Society* (Oct. 1963), p. 150-62.

A gazetteer of the sites around Aden where pottery of archaeological interest has been found.

117 **Socotra: an archaeological reconnaissance in 1967.**

D. Brian Doe. Miami, Florida: Field Research Projects, 1970. 156p. 8 maps. bibliog.

An introduction to the archaeology of the island of Socotra. The main text is a description sector by sector of the archaeology of the island: 1, 'Qallansiya to Ras Habak' (p. 1-39); 2, 'Hadibu to Suk' (p. 39-87); 3, 'Suk to Kalleesa' (p. 87-113); 4, 'Abd al-Kuri Islands' (p. 113-35); and 5, 'Kuria Muria Islands' (p. 135-51). There are notes on pottery, the *Periplus* (see also *The Periplus of the Erythraean Sea* q.v.) and frankincense.

118 **Southern Arabia.**

D. Brian Doe. London: Thames & Hudson, 1971. 267p. bibliog. illus. (New Aspects of Antiquity Series).

An introduction for the general reader to the civilizations and cultures of ancient South Arabia. The book contains excellent plates, including many in colour, and numerous plans and line drawings.

119 **An archaeological journey to Yemen.**
Ahmed Fakhry. Cairo: Government Press, 1951-52. 3 vols. map. bibliog. illus.

In volume 1 the author provides an account of his expedition to the Yemen in 1947 and reproduces his archaeological and architectural drawings and the copies of the pre-Islamic inscriptions that he found. There is also in appendix 1 a brief introduction (in French) to Sabean history and religion by G. Ryckmans. Volume 2 is a scholarly treatment by Ryckmans of the inscriptions found by Fakhry. Volume 3 contains the photographs of the expedition.

120 **Archaeological sites in the Western Aden Protectorate.**
R. A. B. Hamilton. *Geographical Journal*, vol. 101 (Jan.-June 1948), p. 110-17.

A brief survey of possible important archaeological sites in the Western Aden Protectorate.

121 **Pottery and glass fragments from the Aden littoral with historical notes.**
Arthur Lane, R. B. Serjeant. *Journal of the Royal Asiatic Society* (Oct. 1948), p. 108-31.

This publication covers pottery and glass finds in the Aden area and includes notes on the historical background to the discoveries.

122 **Archaeology in the Aden Protectorates.**
C. Lankester Harding. London: HM Stationery Office, 1964. 61p. illus.

A report on the archaeology of South Arabia (present-day People's Democratic Republic of Yemen) with numerous plates and line drawings. The sites are dealt with in Part 2: a list (p. 15-17); and the details (p. 17-49); pre-historic sites are listed (p. 49-50); and Graffiti with notes by A. F. L. Beeston (p. 50-57).

123 **An archaeological and historical survey of the Aden tanks.**
H. T. Norris, F. W. Penhey. Aden: Government Press, 1955. 55p. map.

A study of the water storage tanks of Aden. There is a discussion of the topography of the Aden Peninsula, the discovery of the tanks, the survey of the tanks and their history and origins.

124 **Recently discovered inscriptions and archaeology as sources for ancient South-Arabian kingdoms.**
Jacqueline Pirenne. In: *Studies in the history of Arabia, vol. 1, part 1, Sources for the history of Arabia.* Riyadh: Riyadh University Press, 1979, p. 45-56.

A discussion of the sources used by scholars in their quest to learn more of the pre-Islamic civilization of South Arabia.

Prehistory and Archaeology

125 **Ma'rib dam.**
R. L. Raikes. *Antiquity*, vol. 51 (1977), p. 239-40.

A short article on the famous Ma'rib dam constructed ca. 800 BC and an appeal for a thorough archaeological study.

126 **A bust of a south Arabian winged goddess with nimbus in the possession of Miss Leila Ingrams.**
Jacques Ryckmans. *Arabian Studies*, vol. 3 (1976), p. 67-78.

A study of the pre-Islamic bust of a winged goddess discovered in Bayḥān.

127 **Socotra.**
P. L. Shinnie. *Antiquity*, vol. 34, no. 134 (1960), p. 100-10.

Considers the results of an archaeological reconnaissance in 1956 on the island of Socotra. Includes a map and plans.

128 **Hajar bin Humeid: investigations at a pre-Islamic site in south Arabia.**
Gus W. Van Beek. Baltimore, Maryland: Johns Hopkins Press, 1969. 421p. bibliog. illus. (Publications of the American Foundation for the Study of Man, no. 5).

An archaeological and epigraphic study of the pre-Islamic site of Hajar bin Humeid in Bayḥān. The book contains numerous plates, line drawings and diagrams. There are nine contributors in all, including Gus W. Van Beek, Albert Jamme, Maurice E. Salmon, Thomas R. Soderstrom and William G. Melson.

129 **Early sites of Jabal 'Iyāl Yazīd.**
Robert Wilson. *Arabian Studies*, vol. 4 (1978), p. 67-73.

Provides notes on a number of early sites in the area north of 'Amrān in the Yemen Arab Republic. The notes point to the possible historical and epigraphical interest of each site.

Arabian and Islamic studies.
See item no. 1.

Arabian Studies.
See item no. 17.

Studies in Arabian history and civilisation.
See item no. 19.

Democratic Yemen today.
See item no. 44.

The Oxford University expedition to Socotra.
See item no. 57.

Travels in Yemen.
See item no. 65.

Sheba's daughters: being a record of travel in Southern Arabia.
See item no. 85.

Travels in Arabia.
See item no. 104.

Ḳatabān.
See item no. 136.

Sculptures and inscriptions from Shabwa.
See item no. 145.

Frankincense and myrrh: a study of the Arabian incense trade.
See item no. 147.

Sabaean inscriptions from Maḥram Bilqîs (Mârib).
See item no. 149.

Qataban and Sheba.
See item no. 153.

Cultural policy in the Yemen Arab Republic.
See item no. 367.

The National Museum, Ṣan'ā', YAR.
See item no. 379.

A select bibliography of Yemen Arab Republic and People's Democratic Republic of Yemen.
See item no. 393.

Corpus des inscriptions et antiquités sud-arabes: bibliographie générale systématique. (A collection of writings about South Arabian inscriptions and antiquities: a general systematic bibliography).
See item no. 398.

The Near East (South-west Asia and North Africa): a bibliographic study.
See item no. 401.

History

General

130 **The Islamic dynasties.**
Clifford Edmund Bosworth. Edinburgh: Edinburgh University Press, 1967. 245p. bibliog. (Islamic Surveys, no. 5).

Provides dynastic lists covering the whole of the Islamic world. Chapter 4, 28 the Carmathians, 29 the Zaydī imams, 30 the Sulayhids, and 31 the Rasulids, are of particular relevance.

131 **The historical development of Aden's defences.**
H. T. Norris, F. W. Penhey. *Geographical Journal*, vol. 121, no. 1 (March 1955), p. 11-20.

A history of the defences of Aden since mediaeval times. Includes maps and photographs.

132 **A history of Arabia Felix or Yemen.**
R. L. Playfair. Farnborough, England: Gregg International, 1970. 193p. map. bibliog.

A photo-reproduction of the original Bombay, 1859 edition. The work is a survey of Yemenite history from the beginning of the Christian era down to the 19th century. The author, however, uses few Arabic sources and, although the book is of some value, it should be used with care and discretion.

133 **Yemen.**
A. H. Sharafeddin. Rome: Daily American Press, 1961. 74p.

A work which concentrates on the history of the country from ancient times to the era of the Ḥamīd al-Dīn family in the 20th century.

134 **Laḥdj.**
G. R. Smith. In: *Encyclopaedia of Islam*, Edited by C. E. Bosworth, E. van Donzel, B. Lewis, C. Pellat, Leiden, Netherlands: Brill, 1982. vol. 5, fascicules 87-88, p. 601-02.
A description of the town of Lahej, North of Aden, and its history.

Western Arabia and the Red Sea.
See item no. 4.

Al-Yemen: a general social, political and economic survey.
See item no. 6.

The Middle East: a political and economic survey.
See item no. 11.

The Middle East and North Africa 1981-82.
See item no. 13.

Arabian Studies.
See item no. 17.

Studies in Arabian history and civilisation.
See item no. 19.

Area handbook for the peripheral states of the Arabian Peninsula.
See item no. 20.

The queen of Sheba's land: Yemen (Arabia Felix).
See item no. 21.

Who's who in the Arab world.
See item no. 23.

Yemen Arab Republic: a special report.
See item no. 24.

Yémen. (The Yemen).
See item no. 43.

Democratic Yemen today.
See item no. 44.

In the high Yemen.
See item no. 89.

Notes on Ṣubaiḥī territory, West of Aden.
See item no. 92.

The Jews of Yemen.
See item no. 230.

The Zaydīs.
See item no. 242.

The Saiyids of Ḥaḍramawt.
See item no. 264.

Bibliography on Yemen and notes on Mocha.
See item no. 389.

Theses on Islam, the Middle East and North-west Africa 1880-1978.
See item no. 400.

The Near East (South-west Asia and North Africa): a bibliographic study.
See item no. 401.

Pre-Islamic period (pre-7th century AD)

135 **Epigraphic South Arabian calendars and dating.**
A. F. L. Beeston. London: Luzac, 1956. 47p.

A full discussion of calendars and dating in pre-Islamic South Arabia.

136 **Ḳatabān.**
A. F. L. Beeston. In: *Encyclopaedia of Islam*, Edited by C. E. Bosworth, E. van Donzel, B. Lewis, C. Pellat. Leiden, Netherlands: Brill, 1976. vol. 4, fascicules 71-72, p. 746-48.

An introductory article on the pre-Islamic kingdom of Qatabān in South Arabia which discussed the kingdom's chronology, archaeology and institutions.

137 **Kingship in ancient south Arabia.**
A. F. L. Beeston. *Journal of the Economic and Social History of the Orient*, vol. 15 (1972), p. 256-68.

A study of the social structure of pre-Islamic South Arabia.

138 **New light on the Himyaritic calendar.**
A. F. L. Beeston. *Arabian Studies*, vol. 1 (1974), p. 1-6.

The author provides new information on the pre-Islamic South Arabian calendar in the 4th-6th centuries AD.

139 **Problems of Sabean chronology.**
A. F. L. Beeston. *Bulletin of the School of Oriental and African Studies*, vol. 16, no. 1 (1954), p. 37-56.

Based on epigraphic material, this is a study of the problems of the chronology of the pre-Islamic Sabeans.

140 **Some features of social structure in Saba.**
A. F. L. Beeston. In: *Studies in the History of Arabia*, vol. 1, part 1, *Sources for the history of Arabia.* Riyadh: Riyadh University Press, 1979. p. 115-23.

A study of some aspects of the society of pre-Islamic Saba in South Arabia.

141 **Some observations on Greek and Latin data relating to South Arabia.**
A. F. L. Beeston. *Bulletin of the School of Oriental and African Studies*, vol. 42, no. 1 (1979), p. 7-12.

A brief assessment of the writings of Strabo and Pliny on South Arabia.

142 **Temporary marriage in pre-Islamic south Arabia.**
A. F. L. Beeston. *Arabian Studies*, vol. 4 (1978), p. 21-25.

Some notes on temporary marriage in pre-Islamic South Arabia based on epigraphic texts.

143 **Warfare in ancient south Arabia (2nd-3rd centuries A.D.).**
A. F. L. Beeston. London: Luzac, 1976. 72p. (Qahtan: Studies in old South Arabian Epigraphy, fasc. 3).

A study of warfare and the military campaigns in South Arabia in the pre-Islamic period based on epigraphic texts.

144 **Histoire de Thamoud.** (History of Thamūd.)
A. van den Branden. Beirut: Lebanese University, 1960. 115p. map. bibliog.

Using epigraphic evidence, the author attempts a history of pre-Islamic Thamūd and its inhabitants who travelled and traded widely in the Peninsula.

145 **Sculptures and inscriptions from Shabwa.**
W. L. Brown, A. F. L. Beeston. *Journal of the Royal Asiatic Society*, (April 1954), p. 43-62.

A description of stone fragments and pre-Islamic inscriptions found in Shabwah.

146 **The antiquities of South Arabia.**
Nabib Amin Faris. Princeton, New Jersey: Princeton University Press, 1938. 119p. map.

A translation from Arabic with linguistic, geographic and historical notes of the *Iklīl*, vol. 8, by the tenth century writer al-Ḥasan ḅ Aḥmad al-Hamdānī. The work deals, for example, with the genealogy of the Southern Arabs, the Yemen before Islam, and provides descriptions of the forts and castles.

147 **Frankincense and myrrh: a study of the Arabian incense trade.**
Nigel Groom. London: Longman, 1981. 285p. 8 maps. bibliog.

A comprehensive study of the incense trade in South Arabia. The chapters include: 6, 'The trees and where they grow' (p. 96-121); 9, 'The road through the incense lands' (p. 165-89); and 11, 'Climate and history in Arabia' (p. 214-29).

148 **The Periplus of the Erythraean Sea.**
Translated and edited by G. W. B. Huntingford. London: Hakluyt Society, 1980. 225p. 11 maps. (Hakluyt Society, 2nd ser. no. 151).

A translation from the anonymous geographical Greek text of the 1st or 2nd century AD. The work describes much of everyday life in the Arabian Peninsula including the area of South Arabia. The text also covers India and East Africa.

149 **Sabaean inscriptions from Maḥram Bilqîs (Mârib).**
A. Jamme. Baltimore: Johns Hopkins Press, 1962. 480p. 3 maps. bibliog. illus. (Publications of the American Foundation for the Study of Man, no. 3).

Part 1 of the work contains the texts, translations of, and commentaries on the Mārib inscriptions. Part 2 contains historical studies, notes on pre-Islamic dynasties, genealogical tables, and a chronology of the Sabaean and other kingdoms. There are numerous photographs of the inscriptions and indexes, plus a glossary.

150 **Arabia and the Bible.**
James A. Montgomery. Philadelphia, Pennsylvania: University of Pennsylvania Press, 1934. 207p. map.

A collection of lectures on the Arabian Peninsula and the Bible. The author has chapters on: 6, 'Araby the Blest'; 7, 'South Arabia and the Bible'; 8, 'Relations of Arabia with the history and culture of Palestine' and 'The Sabaeans and Minaeans in the Bible'.

151 **Arabian frankincense in antiquity according to classical sources.**
Walter W. Müller. In *Studies in the History of Arabia*, vol. 1, part 1, *Sources for the history of Arabia.* Riyadh: Riyadh University Press, 1979. p. 79-92.

A study of South Arabian frankincense, its uses and trade in ancient times according to the classical authors.

152 **The background of Islam: being a sketch of Arabian history in pre-Islamic times.**
H. St. J. B. Philby. Alexandria, Egypt: Whitehead Morris, 1947. 152p.

This book has been somewhat overtaken by subsequent publications, although it still remains a work of some value. The author concentrates on the south of the Peninsula.

153 **Qataban and Sheba.**
Wendell Phillips. London: Victor Gollancz, 1955. 335p. 3 maps. illus.

A popular account of the American Foundation for the Study of Man's archaeological expedition to Bayḥān, Mārib and Ẓafār (Dhofar) in the early 1950s. The book has numerous black and white photographs.

154 **A tentative chronological synopsis of the history of Arabia and its neighbours.**
J. W. Redhouse. London: Trubner, 1887. 36p.

A still useful chronological list of events which took place in Arabia, with particular reference to the South, from the earliest times to AD 679.

155 **Les hautes-terres du Nord-Yémen avant l'Islam.** (The highlands of North Yemen before Islam.)
Christian Robin. Istanbul, Turkey: Nederlands Historisch-Archaeologisch Institut, 1982. 2 vols. bibliog.

An examination of the tribal and religious geography of the North of the Yemen in pre-Islamic times.

156 **L'institution monarchique en Arabie méridionale avant l'Islam.** (The institution of the monarchy in pre-Islamic South Arabia.)
Jacques Ryckmans. Louvain: Publications Universitaires and Institut Orientaliste, 1951. 368p. map. bibliog.

A scholarly study of the monarchic institutions of pre-Islamic Maʿīn and Saba in South Arabia. The author discusses the position of both the kings and the *mukarrib* of Saba.

157 **The martyrs of Najrân: new documents.**
Irfan Shahîd. Brussels: Société des Bollandistes, 1971. 306p. bibliog. (Subsidia Hagiographica, no. 49.)

A consideration of the martyrdom of the Christians of Najrān in pre-Islamic times based on new Syriac sources.

History. Pre-Islamic period (pre-7th century AD)

158 **Christianity among the Arabs in pre-Islamic times.**
J. Spencer Trimingham. London, New York: Longman; Beirut: Librairie du Liban, 1979. 342p. 15 maps. bibliog.

The author examines Christianity in the Arabian Peninsula in pre-Islamic times. Chapter 8, 'Christianity in south-west Arabia' (p. 287-208) is of particular relevance.

159 **The rise and fall of Arabia Felix.**
Gus W. Van Beck. *Scientific American*, vol. 221, no. 6 (Dec. 1969), p. 36-58.

The author presents his views on the decline of the pre-Islamic cultures of South Arabia.

Arabian and Islamic studies.
See item no. 1.

Yémen. (The Yemen).
See item no. 9.

Ṣan'ā': an Arabian Islamic city.
See item no. 18.

Travels in Yemen.
See item no. 65.

From Cana (Husn Ghorab) to Sabbatha (Shabwa): the South Arabian incense road.
See item no. 71.

Halévy in Yaman.
See item no. 84.

Sheba's daughters: being a record of travel in Southern Arabia.
See item no. 85.

Some pre-Islamic inscriptions on the frankincense route in Southern Arabia.
See item no. 99.

Arabian and African frankincense trees.
See item no. 107.

Archaeological discoveries in south Arabia.
See item no. 109.

The tombs and Moon Temple of Hureidha (Hadhramaut).
See item no. 110.

An ancient south Arabian necropolis: objects from the second campaign (1951) in the Timna' cemetery.
See item no. 111.

The pre-Islamic antiquities at the Yemen National Museum.
See item no. 112.

Archäologische Berichte aus dem Jemen. (Archaeological reports from the Yemen).
See item no. 113.

Ancient capitals from Aden.
See item no. 114.

Huṣn al-Ġurāb and the site of Qana'.
See item no. 115.

Socotra: an archaeological reconnaissance in 1967.
See item no. 117.

Southern Arabia.
See item no. 118.

An archaeological journey to Yemen.
See item no. 119.

Archaeology in the Aden Protectorates.
See item no. 122.

An archaeological and historical survey of the Aden tanks.
See item no. 123.

Recently discovered inscriptions and archaeology as sources for ancient South-Arabian kingdoms.
See item no. 124.

Ma'rib dam.
See item no. 125.

A bust of a south Arabian winged goddess with nimbus in the possession of Miss Leila Ingrams.
See item no. 126.

Hajar bin Humeid: investigations at a pre-Islamic site in south Arabia.
See item no. 128.

'Adan.
See item no. 168.

Foreign interventions and occupations of Kamarān island.
See item no. 186.

Chronology.
See item no. 200.

Yemen: the politics of the Yemen Arab Republic.
See item no. 302.

North Yemen: images of the built environment.
See item no. 355.

History. Early and Mediaeval Islamic period (7th-18th centuries)

The National Museum, Ṣan'ā', YAR.
See item no. 379.

A select bibliography of Yemen Arab Republic and People's Democratic Republic of Yemen.
See item no. 393.

Corpus des inscriptions et antiquités sud-arabes: bibliographie générale systématique. (A collection of writings about South Arabian inscriptions and antiquities: a general systematic bibliography).
See item no. 398.

Early and Mediaeval Islamic period (7th-18th centuries)

160 **Les débuts de l'imāmat Zaïdite au Yémen.** (The beginnings of the Zaydī imamate in the Yemen.)
C. van Arendonck, translated from the Dutch by Jacques Ryckmans. Leiden, Netherlands: Brill, 1960. 375p. bibliog. (Publications de la Fondation de Goeje, no. 18).

A translation of the original Dutch version which was first published in the same series in 1919. The work is a paraphrase of an autobiography of the first Zaydi imam of the Yemen, al-Hādī ilā 'l-Ḥaqq (d. AD 911). The work is well annotated with some valuable information on, for example, place names and tribal names.

161 **Dinars of al-Mu'aẓẓam Shams al-Dīn Tūrānshāh and al-'Azīz Ṭughtegīn, Ayyubid princes of the Yemen.**
P. Balog. *American Numismatics Society Museum Notes,* vol. 9. (1960), p. 237-40.

A study of some coins of these two Ayyubid rulers of the 12th century Yemen.

162 **Coins of al-Yaman. 132-569 A. H.**
Ramzi J. Bikhazi. *Al-Abḥāth*, vol. 23 (1970), p. 3-127.

The years covered by this extensive numismatic article are AD 749-1173. Although new material has been presented in various different articles since 1970 when this paper was published, the present author lists all Yemeni coins known at that time. It is an invaluable supplement to the early and mediaeval historical information already known.

163 **The collapse of Ottoman authority in Yemen, 968/1560-976/1568.**
J. R. Blackburn. *Die Welt des Islam*, vol. 19 (1979), p. 119-76.

A scholarly account, based mainly on Ottoman sources, which discusses the collapse of Turkish authority in 16th-century Yemen.

164 **The Ottoman penetration of Yemen: an annotated translation of Özdemur Bey's *Fethnâme* for the conquest of Ṣan'ā' in Rajab 954/August 1547.**
J. R. Blackburn. *Archivum Ottomanicum*, vol. 6 (1980), p. 55-100.

This translation of an Ottoman Turkish historical text describes the conquest by the Turks of Ṣan'ā' in 1547.

165 **The diary of a Mocha coffee agent.**
Peter Boxhall. *Arabian Studies*, vol. 1 (1974), p. 102-18.

This diary presents the transactions of an 18th century commissary for affairs of the East India Company in Mocha. The author includes an introduction.

166 **The life and times of Queen Saiyidah Arwā the Ṣulaiḥid of the Yemen.**
Ḥusain F. al-Hamdānī. *Journal of the Royal Central Asian Society*, vol. 31 (1931), p. 505-17.

The text of a lecture delivered to the Society on the 11th-century Yemeni queen, Arwā bint Aḥmad.

167 **Yaman: its early medieval history.**
Henry Cassels Kay. Farnborough, England: Gregg International, 1968. 358p. map.

This is a photo-reproduction of the London, Edward Arnold, 1892, edition, which has been long out of print and unavailable. The great value of the work lies in its annotated translation of an Arabic history of the Yemen from ca. AD 900 to the Ayyubid conquest in the 12th century. There are numerous notes of immense value to the understanding of the early mediaeval history of the area.

168 **'Adan.**
O. Löfgren. In: *Encyclopaedia of Islam.* Edited by H. A. R. Gibb, E. Lévi-Provençal, J. Schacht. Leiden, Netherlands: Brill; London: Luzac, 1957. vol. 1. fascicules 3-4, p. 180-82.

A description of the historic town of Aden, its geography, history, population and buildings are all included.

169 **The Ayyubid dynasty of the Yaman and their coinage.**
G. C. Miles. *Numismatic Chronicle*, vol. 9 (1949), p. 62-97.

A useful survey of the Ayyubid period of mediaeval Yemenite history and a study of some of their coins.

170 **El-Khazreji's history of the Resúlí dynasty of Yemen.**
Edited and translated by James W. Redhouse. Leiden, Netherlands: Brill; London: Luzac, 1906-08. 3 vols. (E. J. W. Gibb Memorial Series, nos. 3/1, 3/2 and 3/3)

These are the first three volumes of a set of five. Volumes 1-2 contain Redhouse's translation of an important Arabic history of the Rasulid dynasty (AD 1228-1454) of the Yemen, a dynasty of unsurpassed brilliance in mediaeval times. Volume 3 contains notes on the translations and volumes 4 and 5 contain the Arabic text.

171 **Political history of the Yemen at the beginning of the sixteenth century.**
Lein Oebele Schuman. Groningen, Netherlands: V. D. R. Kleine, 1960. 142p. map. bibliog.

The translation into English of an Arabic chronicle of the years AD 1500-21. The translation is fully annotated and is of great value in shedding light on early 16th-century Yemenite history. This work provides a good supplement to material found in Robert Bertram Serjeant's *The Portuguese off the South Arabian Coast* (q.v.).

172 **Customary law documents as a source of history.**
R. B. Serjeant. In: *Studies in the history of Arabia, vol. 1, part 2, Sources for the history of Arabia.* Riyadh: Riyadh University Press, 1979. p. 99-103.

An assessment of legal documents as historical sources for the history of the Yemen.

173 **The Portuguese off the South Arabian Coast.**
Robert Bertram Serjeant. Oxford: Clarendon Press, 1963. 233p. 2 maps.

The main section of the book is taken up with annotated translations of the descriptions by Hadrami chroniclers of Portuguese activities in the area of South West Arabia in the very late 15th and 16th centuries. There are lengthy introductions on the political and economic history of the Red Sea and Indian Ocean regions prior to the arrival of the Portuguese and on the general historical background of South West Arabia. The appendixes concern such subjects as shipping terminology and the money and coinage of the time.

174 **Kawkabān: some of its history.**
Clive Smith. *Arabian Studies*, vol. 6 (1982), p. 35.

Provides historical notes on the town of Kawkabān. There is also a plan of the town with notes on its major features.

175 **The Suleihid dynasty in the Yemen.**
Clive K. Smith. *Asian Affairs*, vol. 68 (new series vol. 12) (1981), p. 19-28.

The text of a lecture delivered to the Royal Central Asian Society in 1980. The author briefly studies the mediaeval Ismā'īlī dynasty of the Yemen, the Sulayhids, based in Dhū Jiblah.

176 **The Ayyubids and early Rasulids in the Yemen.**
Gerald Rex Smith. London: E. J. W. Gibb Memorial Trust, 1978. 261p. 2 maps. bibliog. (E. J. W. Gibb Memorial Series, no. 26/2).

This second volume (the first, published under the same English title in 1974, is an edition of an Arabic text chronicling the events of the late 12th and the 13th centuries) is designed to set the historical scene for the Ayyubid and Rasulid dynasty of the Yemen. It also includes a geographical index, a tribal index and a glossary. The Ayyubids (the family of the famous Saladin) prior to their conquest of the Yemen from Egypt are discussed. In addition the scene inside the Yemen is also set and the origins of the Rasulids are also considered.

177 **The Ayyubids and Rasulids: the transfer of power in 7th/13th century Yemen.**
Gerald Rex Smith. *Islamic Culture*, vol. 43. (1969), p. 175-88.

A study of the differing versions offered by the Yemeni mediaeval historians of the transfer of power from the Ayyubids to the Rasulids in 13th-century Yemen.

178 **Ḥadramawt.**
Gerald Rex Smith. In: *Encyclopaedia of Islam*, Edited by C. E. Bosworth, E. van Donzel, B. Lewis, C. Pellat. Leiden, Netherlands: Brill, 1982. Supplement, fascicles 5-6 (1982), p. 337-39.

The author discusses the history, social organization, geography and people of the area.

179 **Ibn Ḥātim's *Kitāb al-Simṭ* and its place in medieval Yemenite historiography.**
G. R. Smith. In: *Studies in the history of Arabia, vol. 1, part 2, Sources for the history of Arabia.* Riyadh, Riyadh University Press, 1979. p. 63-68.

Examines a major source for the history of the Ayyubids in the Yemen in the 12th and 13th centuries.

180 **The Yemenite settlement of Tha'bāt: historical, numismatic and epigraphic notes.**
Gerald Rex Smith. *Arabian Studies*, vol. 1 (1974), p. 119-34.

Provides notes on the history, coins and inscriptions of Tha'bāt, a settlement near Ta'izz.

181 **Arab navigation in the Indian Ocean before the coming of the Portuguese.**
G. R. Tibbetts. London: Royal Asiatic Society, 1971. 614p. 6 maps. bibliog. (Oriental Translation fund, new series, no. 42).

The bulk of the work is taken up with a translation of a 15th century treatise on Indian Ocean navigation by Aḥmad b. Mājid al-Najdī. There is an introduction to the history of Arab navigation and notes on navigational techniques and on Indian Ocean topography. The volume contains a great deal of information concerning the Red Sea coast of the Yemen, as well as the Southern Indian Ocean coast and the islands.

182 **Arabia in the fifteenth century navigational texts.**
G. R. Tibbetts. *Arabian Studies*, vol. 1 (1974), p. 86-101.

A study of the Southern and Eastern coasts and coastal towns of the Arabian Peninsula in the late mediaeval period.

183 **The rise of the imams of Sanaa.**
A. S. Tritton. Oxford: Oxford University Press, 1925. 141p.

This is a history of the Yemeni uprisings against the Turkish occupiers in the late 16th and 17th centuries. The account relies on Yemenite Arabic sources of the time.

Yémen. (The Yemen).
See item no. 9.

Ṣan'ā': an Arabian Islamic city.
See item no. 18.

Atlas of Islamic history.
See item no. 38.

A journey by two Jesuits from Dhufar to Ṣan'ā' in 1590.
See item no. 49.

Archäologische Berichte aus dem Jemen. (Archaeological reports from the Yemen).
See item no. 113.

Pottery sites near Aden.
See item no. 116.

Socotra: an archaeological reconnaissance in 1967.
See item no. 117.

Pottery and glass fragments from the Adan littoral with historical notes.
See item no. 121.

An archaeological and historical survey of the Aden tanks.
See item no. 123.

The historical development of Aden's defences.
See item no. 131.

The antiquities of South Arabia.
See item no. 146.

A tentative chronological synopsis of the history of Arabia and its neighbours.
See item no. 154.

Foreign interventions and occupations of Kamarān island.
See item no. 186.

Chronology.
See item no. 200.

Yemen: the politics of the Yemen Arab Republic.
See item no. 302.

Notes on the development of Zaidi law.
See item no. 312.

Histoire du commerce entre le Levant et l'Europe. (The history of trade between Europe and the East).
See item no. 338.

Islam and the trade of Asia: a colloquium.
See item no. 339.

The cultivation of cereals in medieval Yemen.
See item no. 347.

North Yemen: images of the built environment.
See item no. 355.

Three medieval mosques in the Yemen.
See item no. 359.

Two early mosques in the Yemen: a preliminary report.
See item no. 360.

Architecture of the Islamic world; its history and social meaning.
See item no. 361.

Conservation in Yemen.
See item no. 362.

Mathematical astronomy in medieval Yemen.
See item no. 371.

Arabic and Turkish source materials for the early history of Ottoman Yemen, 945/1538-976/1568.
See item no. 385.

A select bibliography of Yemen Arab Republic and People's Democratic Republic of Yemen.
See item no. 393.

Corpus des inscriptions et antiquités sud-arabes: bibliographie générale systématique. (A collection of writings about South Arabian inscriptions and antiquities: a general systematic bibliography).
See item no. 398.

Modern period (19th-20th centuries)

184 **Notes towards an understanding of the revolution in South Yemen.**
Hussein Ali, Ken Whittingham. *Race and Class*, vol. 16, no. 1 (July 1974), p. 83-100.

The author provides background material concerning events leading up to the withdrawal of the British from Aden in 1967.

185 **British naval operations against Turkish Yaman 1914-1919.**
John Baldry. *Arabica*, vol. 25, no. 2 (June 1978), p. 148-97.

An history of British operations against the Turks in the Yemen in the 20th century.

186 **Foreign interventions and occupations of Kamarān island.**
John Baldry. *Arabian Studies*, vol. 4 (1978), p. 89-111.

A study of the foreign occupations of the Yemeni Red Sea island of Kamarān from pre-Islamic times to the present day.

187 **Imām Yaḥyā and the Yamanī uprising of 1911.**
John Baldry. *Annali Istituto Orientale di Napoli*, vol. 42, no. 3 (1982), p. 425-59.

The author considers the background to the Yemeni revolt against the Turks and the Siege of Ṣan'ā' in 1911.

188 **The Turkish-Italian war in the Yemen 1911-1912.**
John Baldry. *Arabian Studies*, vol. 3 (1976), p. 51-65.

An account, based on official documents, of the Turkish-Italian war in North West Yemen.

189 **Al-Yaman and the Turkish occupation 1849-1914.**
John Baldry. *Arabica*, vol. 23 (1976), p. 156-96.

An historical examination of the Turkish occupation of the Yemen in the 19th and 20th centuries.

190 **The Yamani island of Kamaran during the Napoleonic wars.**
John Baldry. *Middle Eastern Studies*, vol. 16 (Oct. 1980), p. 246-66.

An historical study of the Red Sea island of Kamarān in Napoleonic times.

191 **The political residents of Aden: biographical notes.**
Robin Bidwell. *Arabian Studies*, vol. 5 (1979), p. 149-59.

The author supplies biographical notes on all the British political residents of Aden from S. B. Haines (1839) to Bernard Reilly (1940).

192 **The Turkish attack on Aden 1915-1918.**
Robin Bidwell. *Arabian Studies*, vol. 6 (1982), p. 171-94.

A consideration of the Turkish attack on British Aden during the First World War.

193 **The two Yemens.**
Robin Bidwell. Harlow, England: Longman; Boulder, Colorado: Westview Press, 1983. 350p. map. bibliog.

A history of the two countries since the time of European intervention in the area in the 16th century. An authoritative book by an author who served in the British administration of the Western Aden Protectorate. The chapters include: 2, 'European intervention . . . ' (p. 16-34); 3, 'Two empires in the Yemen' (p. 36-59); 4, 'Aden and the hinterland' (p. 66-84); 5, 'Yemen under the Mutawakilite kings 1919-1962' (p. 104-21); 6, 'The Federation of South Arabia' (p. 130-84); 7, 'The war in the North 1962-70' (p. 195-219); 8, 'The two Yemens 1968-72' (p. 219-55); 9, 'The two Yemens 1972-79' (p. 262-314); and 'Postscript: March 1979 to October 1981' (p. 321-38).

194 **British imperialism in southern Arabia.**
New York: Research Section, Arab Information Center, 1958. 86p. map. (Information Papers, no. 6.)

Only part 1 is of relevance here. It is entitled 'British penetration and imperialism in Yemen' by Fathalla El Khatib and Khalid I. Babaa. The tone throughout is aggressively anti-British.

195 **Arabia: when Britain goes.**
Fabian Society. London: Fabian Society, 1967. 28p. map. (Fabian Research Series, no. 259.)

South Arabia and Yemen appear first in the list of countries and areas of the Arabian Peninsula affected by the withdrawal of the British from these countries and areas in the 1960s and 1970s.

196 **The Yemen revisited.**
Christopher Gandy. *Asian Affairs*, vol. 58 (new series vol. 2) (1971), p. 295-304.

The text of a talk delivered at the Royal Central Asian Society in London in 1971 by the former British Minister in Ta'izz in 1962-63. The author traces the history of the Yemen since the 1962 revolution and assesses the problems then facing the country.

197 **Aden under British rule: 1839-1967.**
R. J. Gavin. London: Hurst, 1975. 472p. 4 maps. bibliog.

An history of the British in Aden based on government records and documents. The chapters include: 1, 'The British come to Aden' (p. 1-39); 2, 'Aden under Haines' (p. 39-62); 5, 'Turkish intervention and the beginning of the Protectorate' (p. 131-56); 6, 'The Hadhrami sultanates 1800-1900' (p. 156-74); 8, 'Anglo-Turkish relations and the delimitation of the Yemeni boundary' (p. 195-227); and 12, 'Apogee and evacuation' (p. 318-52).

198 **The conspirators.**
Scott Gibbons. London: Howard Baker, 1967. 192p.

An indictment of Egyptian policy towards the Yemen and of both Gamal Abd el-Nasser's aims in the area and his participation in the civil war which followed the 1962 revolution.

199 **Arabia without sultans.**
Fred Halliday. Harmondsworth, England: Penguin Books, 1974. 527p. 16 maps. bibliog.

A study of the Arabian Peninsula after British withdrawal from the area. Part 2 deals with the Yemen Arab Republic and part 3 with the People's Democratic Republic of Yemen. The chapters include, part 2: 3, 'The Imamate and its contradictions' (p. 81-96); 4, 'Civil war and counter-revolution' (p. 101-22); 5, 'The counter-revolutionary state' (p. 131-45); and part 3: 6, 'South Yemen under British rule' (p. 153-69); 7, 'The liberation movement 1953-67' (p. 178-214); and 8, 'The People's Democratic Republic of Yemen' (p. 227-58).

200 **Chronology.**
Jane Smiley Hart. *Middle East Journal*, vol. 17, nos. 1 and 2 (winter-spring 1963), p. 104-43.

A general chronology of the Middle East, 1962-63, which covers: Aden, p. 105-07; the UAR (including Yemen), p. 139-41; and the Yemen, p. 141-43. There is also a supplement to the article entitled a 'Basic chronology for a history of the Yemen', p. 144-53.

201 **The Yemen.**
J. Heyworth-Dunne. *Middle Eastern Affairs*, vol. 9, no. 2 (Feb. 1958), p. 50-58.

A brief description of the Yemen of the 1950s.

202 **Aden.**
Sir Tom Hickinbotham. London: Constable, 1958. 242p. map.

A personal account of Aden in the 1940s and 1950s by an ex-chairman of the Aden Port Trust and an ex-Governor.

203 **Farewell to Arabia.**
David Holden. London: Faber & Faber, 1966. 268p. 3 maps. bibliog.

The early chapters of the book concern the Yemen and trace her modern history down to the 1962 revolution.

204 **The Yemen: imams, rulers and revolutions.**
Harold Ingrams. London: John Murray, 1963. 164p. map.

The events leading up to the 1962 revolution in the Yemen are told by the one-time British Resident Adviser in the Western Aden Protectorate. Anglo-Yemeni relations comprise a large section of the book.

205 **Kings of Arabia: the rise and set of the Turkish sovranty in the Arabian Peninsula. (sic.)**
Harold F. Jacob. London: Mills & Boon, 1923. 294p. bibliog.

The author, Resident Agent in the Aden hinterland, chronicles the events of Turkish involvement in South West Arabia; events in which he was personally much involved.

206 **The view from Steamer Point: being an account of three years in Aden.**
Charles Hepburn Johnston. London: Collins, 1964. 224p. map.

A personal account of events in South Arabia during the years 1960-63, when the author was firstly Governor and later High Commissioner for Aden and the Protectorates. These years saw the negotiations to merge Aden Colony into the Federation of South Arabia and the author was personally involved in them.

207 **The first days of British Aden: the diary of John Studdy Leigh.**
James Kirkman, Brian Doe. *Arabian Studies*, vol. 2 (1975), p. 179-203.

An edition, with an introduction, of the diary of a young Englishman who arrived in Aden in 1838 as supercargo on a trading vessel. His arrival coincided with the operations which resulted in the British occupation. This diary provides much interesting information about the period.

208 **Arab radical politics: al-Qawniyyūn al-'Arab and the Marxists in the turmoil of South Yemen, 1963-1967.**
Joseph Kostiner. *Middle Eastern Studies*, vol. 17 (Oct. 1981), p. 454-76.

A study of the political and social history of South Arabia up to the time of independence in 1967 and the creation of the People's Democratic Republic of Yemen.

209 **The history of Aden.**
Z. H. Kour. London: Frank Cass, 1981. 240p. 3 maps. bibliog.

A history of Aden after the arrival of the British in the area. The author devotes individual chapters to three 19th-century Arab rulers of Aden. The chapters include: 2, 'The growth of the settlement' (p. 13-63); 3, 'Trade' (p. 63-77); 4, 'The administration' (p. 77-105); 5, 'Sultan Muhsin' (p. 105-40); 6, 'Sultan 'Ali' (p. 140-89); and 7, 'Sultan Fadl' (p. 189-219).

210 **Why the British took Aden.**
Zaki Kour. *Middle East International,* (Feb. 1976), p. 28-29.

A brief article for the general reader which sets out the author's interpretation of the reasons for the British occupation of Aden in 1839.

211 **South Arabia: arena of conflict.**
Tom Little. London: Pall Mall Press, 1968. 196p. 3 maps. bibliog.

An account of the more recent history of Aden and the hinterland down to the birth of the People's Democratic Republic of Yemen. The chapters include: 3, 'The Arab Amirates of the South' (p. 36-68); 4, 'The Aden merger' (p. 68-100); 5, 'The start of the struggle' (p. 100-20); 6, 'The embryo state' (p. 120-39); 8, 'Britain's volte face' (p. 148-61); and 10, 'Birth of the republic' (p. 174-87).

212 **Fremantle at Aden in *H.M.S. Challenger* 1830.**
Eric Macro. *Arabian Studies,* vol. 6 (1982), p. 211-12.

Notes on British naval activity in the Indian Ocean before the British occupation of Aden. Particular attention is paid to the role of Charles Howe Fremantle, commander of the *Challenger.*

213 **The war in the Yemen.**
Edgar O'Ballance. London: Faber & Faber, 1971. 218p. 2 maps. bibliog.

Provides the background to, and an account of, the civil war in the Yemen after the 1962 revolution. The chapters include: 2, 'Imam Ahmed' (43-65); 3, 'Revolution' (p. 65-79); 9, 'The Harad conference' (p. 153-71); 10, 'The fall of as-Sallal' (p. 171-89); and 11, 'The siege of Sana' (p. 189-203).

214 **Last post: Aden 1964-1967.**
Julian Paget. London: Faber & Faber, 1969. 279p. 5 maps.

A history of the last years of British involvement in Aden.

215 **Armies of the Middle East.**
Otto van Pivka. Cambridge: Patrick Stephens, 1979. 169p.

The author provides information from non-official sources on uniforms, weapons, equipment and campaign history. The first section includes the Yemen civil war 1962-69. Section 3 deals briefly with armed forces, including the para-military forces, of the Yemen Arab Republic and the People's Democratic Republic of Yemen.

216 **The Arabian Peninsula.**
Richard H. Sanger. Ithaca, New York: Cornell University Press, 1954. bibliog.

The author describes much of the Arabian Peninsula in the early 1950s. Chapters 15-19 concern Aden, the Protectorate and the Yemen.

217 **Yemen: the unknown war.**
Dana Adams Schmidt. London, Sydney, Toronto: Bodley Head, 1968. 316p. 2 maps.

An examination of the civil war in the Yemen after the revolution of 1962.

218 **The two Yemens: historical perspectives and present attitudes.**
Robert Bertram Serjeant. *Asian Affairs*, vol. 60. (Feb. 1973), p. 3-17.

A survey of the modern history of both countries, with particular reference to the 1962 Yemen revolution and events leading to independence in Aden in 1967.

219 **Documents on the history of southwest Arabia: tribal warfare and foreign policy in Yemen, Aden and adjacent tribal kingdoms, 1920-29.**
Edited by Reginald W. Sinclair. Salisbury, North Carolina: Documentary Publications, 1976. 2 vols. 8 maps.

A collection of photographically reproduced US documents concerning the political history of the area in the 1920s.

220 **Notes on the Kathiri state of Hadhramaut.**
R. H. Smith. *Middle East Journal*, vol. 7, no. 4 (Autumn 1953), p. 499-503.

Brief historical, political and commercial notes on the Kathīrī state in the 1950s.

221 **Shades of Amber: a South Arabian episode.**
Sir Kennedy Trevaskis. London: Hutchinson, 1968. 256p. map.

A consideration of the years 1951-67 in South Arabia. The author was latterly British High Commissioner in the area.

222 **Sultans of Aden.**
Gordon Waterfield. London: John Murray, 1968. 267p. 3 maps.

The author discusses Aden after the arrival of the British in the area in 1837. The book concentrates in particular on the leading British figure of the time, Captain S. B. Haines. Amongst the chapters included in the volume are: 2, 'The East India Company and steam navigation' (p. 11-19); 2, 'Haines recommends Aden as a coaling station' (p. 19-32); 4, 'Sultan Mahsin of Lahej sells Aden to the British' (p. 37-47); 8, 'The British take Aden by storm' (p. 70-79); 20, 'Death of Sultan Mahsin of Lahej' (p. 196-205); 21, 'Haines is dismissed' (p. 205-14); 22, 'Mystery of the missing funds' (p. 214-24); 23, 'Trial and acquittal' (p. 224-30); and 25, 'Freedom and death' (p. 239-43).

223 **Modern Yemen 1918-1966.**
Manfred W. Wenner. Baltimore, Maryland: Johns Hopkins Press, 1967. 257p. map. bibliog. (The Johns Hopkins University Studies in Historical and Political Science, no. 85/1).

The author divides his work into three parts: Arabia Felix; internal affairs; and external affairs. There is brief introductory material on the Yemen under the Ottomans from the 1840s. External affairs includes Yemeni-Saudi relations and 'Asīr and Anglo-Yemeni relations and Aden.

Arabian and Islamic studies.
See item no. 1.

An account of the British settlement of Aden in Arabia.
See item no. 7.

Yémen. (The Yemen).
See item no. 9.

Ṣan'ā': an Arabian Islamic city.
See item no. 18.

Atlas of Islamic history.
See item no. 38.

Dutch travellers in Arabia in the seventeenth century. Parts I and II.
See item no. 48.

A journey by two Jesuits from Dhufar to Ṣan'ā' in 1590.
See item no. 49.

Some early travels in Arabia.
See item no. 50.

The kingdom of Melchior: adventure in south west Arabia.
See item no. 51.

The uneven road.
See item no. 52.

Yémen 62-69: de la révolution 'sauvage' à la trève des guerriers. (The Yemen 62-69: from the 'savage' revolution to the warriors' truce).
See item no. 60.

A French family in the Yemen.
See item no. 62.

A visit to the Idrisi territory in 'Asir and Yemen.
See item no. 63.

The exploration of the Aden Protectorate.
See item no. 72.

Perfumes of Araby: silhouettes of al-Yemen.
See item no. 73.

The barren rocks of Aden.
See item no. 75.

The war in the Yemen.
See item no. 76.

El Yemen: tre anni nell' Arabia Felice. (Yemen: three years in Arabia Felix).
See item no. 79.

The Yemen in 1937-38.
See item no. 91.

Arabian assignment.
See item no. 93.

A modern pilgrim in Mecca and a siege in Sanaa.
See item no. 103.

'Adan.
See item no. 168.

Customary law documents as a source of history.
See item no. 172.

Political conflict and stratification in Ḥaḍramaut.
See item no. 245.

The politics of stratification.
See item no. 246.

Burke's Royal families of the world. Vol. II. Africa and the Middle East.
See item no. 247.

A time in Arabia.
See item no. 254.

The Hadramaut in time of war.
See item no. 255.

The Hadramaut: present and future.
See item no. 256.

The Free Yemeni Movement (1940-48) and its ideas on reform.
See item no. 272.

Aden and the Arab South.
See item no. 273.

Army officers in Arab politics and society.
See item no. 274.

South Arabia: violence and revolt.
See item no. 275.

Soviet uses of proxies in the Third World: the case of Yemen.
See item no. 276.

The Yemeni dilemma.
See item no. 277.

Urban élites and colonialism: the nationalist élites of Aden and South Arabia.
See item no. 278.

The emergence of Aden since 1956.
See item no. 279.

Revolutions and military rule in the Middle East: the Arab states; part II. Egypt, the Sudan, Yemen and Libya.
See item no. 281.

Arabia and the isles.
See item no. 284.

Political development in the Hadhramaut.
See item no. 285.

Peace in the Hadramaut.
See item no. 286.

The problems of South-west Arabia.
See item no. 287.

Hadramaut, Oman, Dhufar: the experience of revolution.
See item no. 288.

Coup and counter-coup in the Yaman 1948.
See item no. 289.

Imperial outpost-Aden: its place in British strategic policy.
See item no. 290.

The problem of Aden.
See item no. 291.

Kuwayt and Aden: a contrast in British policies.
See item no. 293.

The Yemen Arab Republic and the politics of balance.
See item no. 294.

Yemen: the search for a modern state.
See item no. 295.

Aden and the Yemen.
See item no. 296.

Political dictionary of the Middle East in the twentieth century.
See item no. 299.

Social structure and politics in the Yemen Arab Republic.
See item no. 300.

South Yemen: a Marxist republic in Arabia.
See item no. 301.

Yemen: the politics of the Yemen Arab Republic.
See item no. 302.

Specialist revolution in Arabia: a report from the People's Democratic Republic of Yemen.
See item no. 303.

The Middle East in revolution.
See item no. 304.

Arab politics in the United Nations.
See item no. 305.

Ingrams' peace in Hadhramaut.
See item no. 306.

The Yemeni constitution and its religious orientation.
See item no. 307.

A constitution for South Arabia.
See item no. 308.

Aden and the Federation of South Arabia.
See item no. 309.

History. Modern period (19th-20th century)

Yemen: political history, social structure and legal system.
See item no. 311.

Constitutions of the countries of the world: People's Democratic Republic of Yemen.
See item no. 313.

Constitutions of the countries of the world: Yemen Arab Republic.
See item no. 314.

Resolution of the Yemen crisis, 1963: a case study in mediation.
See item no. 318.

Yemen and the Western world.
See item no. 319.

Great Britain's relations with Yemen and Oman.
See item no. 320.

Conflict in the Yemens and superpower involvement.
See item no. 321.

Le sous-développement économique et social du Yémen: perspectives de la révolution Yémenite. (Economic and social underdevelopment in the Yemen: aspects of the Yemeni revolution).
See item no. 324.

Emigration and economic development: the case of the Yemen Arab Republic.
See item no. 331.

Histoire du commerce entre le Levant et l'Europe. (The history of trade between Europe and the East).
See item no. 338.

Labor relations and trades unions in Aden 1952-1960.
See item no. 353.

North Yemen: images of the built environment.
See item no. 355.

A select bibliography of Yemen Arab Republic and People's Democratic Republic of Yemen.
See item no. 393.

Corpus des inscriptions et antiquités sud-arabes: bibliographie générale systématique. (A collection of writings about South Arabian inscriptions and antiquities: a general systematic bibliography).
See item no. 398.

Population

224 **Fertility, mortality, migration and family planning in the Yemen Arab Republic.**
J. Allman, A. G. Hill. *Population Studies*, vol. 32, no. 1 (March 1978), p. 159-71.

A statistical study of population and family planning in the Yemen Arab Republic.

225 **People's Democratic Republic of Yemen: report on needs assessment for population assistance.**
New York: United Nations Fund for Population Activities, 1978. map.

A report which resulted from a mission in 1977 to consider population assistance in the People's Democratic Republic of Yemen. The section headings are as follows: 'National setting'; 'Basic population data and needs'; 'Population dynamics and policy formulation'; 'Manpower situation and requirements'; 'Strategies affecting population, settlement schemes'; 'Health programmes and population education'; 'External assistance'; and 'Recommendations for population assistance'.

226 **Les Yémens et leurs populations.** (The Yemens and their populations.)
Alain Rouaud. Brussels: Editions complexe, 1979. 204p. map. bibliog. (Pays et Populations Series.)

A study of the different peoples of the two Yemens.

227 **A contribution to the population geography of the Yemen Arab Republic.**
Hans Steffen. Wetzikon, Switzerland: Druckerei Wetzikon, 1979. 179p. and 132p. 19 maps. bibliog.

A PhD dissertation submitted to the University of Zurich. The work incorporates the major findings of the population and housing census of February 1975 and the supplementary demographic and cartographic surveys carried out in the districts of Turbat al-Shama'itayn, Jabal 'Iyāl Yazīd and al-Suhayyah.

228 **Democratic Yemen.**
United Nations Economic Commission for Western Asia. Beirut: United Nations Economic Commission for Western Asia, 1980. map. bibliog. (The Population Situation in the ECWA Region.)

A detailed analysis of population statistics in the People's Democratic Republic of Yemen.

229 **Yemen.**
United Nations Economic Commission for Western Asia. Beirut: United Nations Economic Commission for Western Asia, 1979. map. bibliog. (The Population Situation in the ECWA Region).

A detailed analysis of population statistics in the Yemen Arab Republic.

Al-Yemen: a general social, political and economic survey.
See item no. 6.

An account of the British settlement of Aden in Arabia.
See item no. 7.

Survey of social and economic conditions in the Aden protectorate.
See item no. 8.

The Middle East: a political and economic survey.
See item no. 11.

Area handbook for the peripheral states of the Arabian Peninsula.
See item no. 20.

Population distribution, administrative division and land use in the Yemen Arab Republic.
See item no. 34.

'Adan.
See item no. 168.

Women's status and fertility in the Muslim world.
See item no. 243.

Some consequences of emigration for rural economic development in Yemen Arab Republic.
See item no. 332.

Asia.
See item no. 340.

Yemen Arab Republic.
See item no. 346.

U.N. Statistical Yearbook.
See item no. 354.

Minorities

230 **The Jews of Yemen.**
S. D. Goitein. In: *Religion in the Middle East,* vol. 1, *Judaism and Christianity.* Edited by A. J. Arberry. Cambridge, England: Cambridge University Press, 1969. p. 226-39.

The author deals briefly with the history of the Jewish community in the Yemen, the great majority of whom had migrated to Israel by 1962. He then describes the economic and social conditions of the Jews in the Yemen and their particular brand of Judaism.

231 **A Judeo-Arab house-deed from Ḥabbān (with notes of the former Jewish communities of the Wāḥidī Sultanate).**
R. B. Serjeant. *Journal of the Royal Asiatic Society,* (Oct. 1953), p. 117-131.

The text and a translation of a Jewish South Arabia house-deed with notes on the Jewish community of the Wāḥidī Sultanate and a glossary of technical terms.

Ṣan'ā': an Arabian Islamic city.
See item no. 18.

Yémen 62-69: de la révolution 'sauvage' à la trève des guerriers. (The Yemen 62-69: from the 'savage' revolution to the warriors' truce).
See item no. 60.

Travels in Yemen.
See item no. 65.

The martyrs of Najrân: new documents.
See item no. 157.

Christianity among the Arabs in pre-Islamic times.
See item no. 158.

The language of al-Gades. The main characteristics of an Arabic dialect spoken in Lower Yemen.
See item no. 236.

Jewish domestic architecture in Ṣan'ā', Yemen.
See item no. 363.

Overseas Populations

232 **Detroit's Yemeni workers.**
Nabeel Abraham. *Middle East Research and Information Project Reports,* Report no. 57 (May, 1977), p. 3-9.

A social and economic study of the Yemeni migrant workers in the Detroit car industry.

233 **Aspects of labour migration from North Yemen.**
J. S. Birks, C. A. Sinclair, J. A. Stocknat. *Middle Eastern Studies,* vol. 17 (Jan. 1981), p. 49-63.

An economic study of temporary migration abroad by citizens of the Yemen Arab Republic. It includes a discussion of the number and significance of the Yemenis working abroad and the impact of such migration.

Language and Dialects

234 **Skizzen jemenitischer Dialekte.** (Sketches of Yemeni dialects.)
Werner Diem. Beirut; Wiesbaden, GFR: Franz Steiner, 1973. 166p. map. bibliog. (Beiruter Texte und Studien, no. 13.)

A scholarly study of certain Yemeni Arabic dialects, including those of ʻAmrān, Yarīm, Dhamār, Taʻizz and Ibb.

235 **Aden Arabic for beginners.**
Muhammad Abduh Ghanem. Aden, 1958. 2nd ed. 178p.

A basic manual of the Arabic dialect of Aden. The presentation is based on conversations, followed by a vocabulary, grammatic notes and exercises.

236 **The language of al-Gades. The main characteristics of an Arabic dialect spoken in Lower Yemen.**
S. D. Goitein. *Le Muséon*, vol. 73 (1960), p. 351-94.

A study of the Arabic dialect of the Jewish village of al-Gades near Ibb. The author provides annotated and translated texts in the dialect.

237 **A sketch of the Arabic dialect of the central Yamani Tihāmah.**
Joseph Greenman. *Zeitschrift für arabische Linguistik*, vol. 3, no. 3 (1979), p. 47-61.

A study of the Arabic dialect of the Tihāmah region of the Yemen Arab Republic, including the towns of Zabīd and Hodeida.

238 **Arabic simplified.**
Khan Saheb Syed Hamood Hason. Aden: published by the author, 1919. 964p.

A still useful manual of Adeni colloquial and written Arabic. Sentences and examples are presented under various subjects. There is a vocabulary and a short grammatical introduction.

Language and Dialects

239 **Études sur les dialectes de l'Arabie méridionale.** (Studies on the dialects of Southern Arabia.)
Comte de Landberg. Leiden, Netherlands: Brill, 1901-13. 2 vols.

The author provides translations of, and commentaries on, South Arabian colloquial literature, prose and poetry. The texts throw much light on everyday life and social conditions in South Arabia in the late 19th and early 20th century. Vol. I is sub-titled 'Ḥaḍramoût', and Volume 2, in two parts, 'Daṯînah'.

240 **Glossaire Daṯînois.**
Comte de Landberg. Leiden, Netherlands: Brill, 1920-42. 3 vols.

A glossary of the Arabic dialects of South Arabia. The work is of some relevance for the whole area and 'Dathinan' need not be taken too literally here.

241 **L'Arabo parlato a Ṣan'ā'.**
Ettore Rossi. Rome: Istituto per l'Oriente, 1939. 250p.

A study of the grammar of the Arabic dialect of Ṣan'ā'. The work includes texts and a glossary.

Arabian and Islamic studies.
See item no. 1.

Al-Yemen: a general social, political and economic survey.
See item no. 6.

Survey of social and economic conditions in the Aden protectorate.
See item no. 8.

Ṣan'ā': an Arabian Islamic city.
See item no. 18.

Travels in Yemen.
See item no. 65.

Arabica.
See item no. 74.

The Ayyubids and early Rasulids in the Yemen.
See item no. 176.

Asia.
See item no. 340.

Theses on Islam, the Middle East and North-west Africa 1880-1978.
See item no. 400.

The Near East (South-west Asia and North Africa): a bibliographic study.
See item no. 401.

Religion

242 **The Zaydīs.**
R. B. Serjeant. In: *Religion in the Middle East,* vol. 2, *Islam.* Edited by A. J. Arberry. Cambridge, England: Cambridge University Press, 1969. p. 285-302.

The author deals primarily with the Zaydiyyah as a religious group of the Shī'ah. He also discusses the Zaydīs within Yemeni society through the ages.

Arabia and Islamic studies.
See item no. 1.

An account of the British settlement of Aden in Arabia.
See item no. 7.

Survey of social and economic conditions in the Aden protectorate.
See item no. 8.

The Middle East: a political and economic survey.
See item no. 11.

Area handbook for the peripheral states of the Arabian Peninsula.
See item no. 20.

The queen of Sheba's land: Yemen (Arabia Felix).
See item no. 21.

Atlas of Islamic history.
See item no. 38.

An archaeological journey to Yemen.
See item no. 119.

Les hautes-terres du Nord-Yémen avant l'Islam. (The highlands of North Yemen before Islam).
See item no. 155.

The martyrs of Najrân: new documents.
See item no. 157.

Christianity among the Arabs in pre-Islamic times.
See item no. 158.

Ḥadramawt.
See item no. 178.

Das Qāt. (Qat).
See item no. 261.

The 'White Dune' at Abyan: an ancient place of pilgrimage in Southern Arabia.
See item no. 266.

Yemen: the politics of the Yemen Arab Republic.
See item no. 302.

The Yemeni constitution and its religious orientation.
See item no. 307.

Notes on the development of Zaidi law.
See item no. 312.

Asia.
See item no. 340.

Architecture of the Islamic world; its history and social meaning.
See item no. 361.

Folklore and folk literature in Oman and Socotra.
See item no. 377.

The status of the Arab woman: a select bibliography.
See item no. 392.

Corpus des inscriptions et antiquités sud-arabes: bibliographie générale systématique. (A collection of writings about South Arabian inscriptions and antiquities: a general systematic bibliography).
See item no. 398.

Social Conditions and Organization

243 **Women's status and fertility in the Muslim world.**
Edited by James Allman. New York, London: Praeger, 1978. 287p. (Praeger Special Studies.)

A collection of essays on demographic change, family planning, changing family patterns and women's status. The entire Middle East is covered. Chapter 16 deals with women and social change in urban North Yemen.

244 **Some observations on Yemeni food habits.**
Annika Bornstein. *Nutrition Newsletter*, vol. 10, no. 3 (July-Sept. 1972), p. 1-9.

A description of the eating habits of Yemenis which attempts to establish the economic and social reasons behind these habits. The author also discusses the steps being taken towards modifying and improving eating habits.

245 **Political conflict and stratification in Ḥaḍramaut.**
A. S. Bujra. *Middle Eastern Studies*, vol. 3, no. 4 (July 1967), p. 355-76; vol. 4, no. 1 (Oct. 1967), p. 2-29.

A study of the politics of Ḥaḍramawt in the 1960s and the effect of the Yemeni revolution on Ḥaḍrami society.

246 **The politics of stratification.**
Abdalla S. Bujra. Oxford: Clarendon Press, 1971. 201p. map. bibliog.

The author here discusses political change in the Ḥaḍrami town of Ḥurayḍah. The book analyses the rigid stratification which the author found in the society of the town which was composed of three rigid social classes: the *sādah*; the *mashāyikh* and tribesmen; and the *masākin* (the 'poor') the lowest stratum.

247 **Burke's Royal families of the world. Vol. II. Africa and the Middle East.**
London: Burke's Peerage Limited, 1980. 271p.

This volume provides the pedigrees and genealogy of royal families in two continents. It contains a brief summary of early Yemeni rulers and includes details of imams of Yemen from 1891 to the time of the republican coup in 1962. The work also contains a survey of the small sultanates, amirates and shaikdoms of the former Aden Protectorates up to the establishment of the People's Republic of South Yemen in 1967. The People's Democratic Republic of Yemen is dealt with on p. 1-7 and the Yemen Arab Republic on p. 256-7.

248 **Sozio-ökonomische Aspekt der Stammesdemokratie in Nordost-Yemen.** (Socio-economic aspects of tribal democracy in north-east Yemen.)
Walter Dostal. *Sociologus*, vol. 24, no. 1 (1974), p. 1-15.

A study in German (with an English synopsis) of tribal democracy and the economic conditions for tribal autonomy with particular reference to Banū Ḥushaysh.

249 **Market, mosque and mafraj: social inequality in a Yemeni town.**
Tomas Gerholm. Stockholm: University of Stockholm, 1977. 217p. 2 maps. bibliog. (Stockholm Studies in Social Anthropology, no. 5.)

A social anthropological study of the town of Manākhah in the Yemen Arab Republic.

250 **The social organisation of the tribes of the Aden Protectorate.**
R. A. B. Hamilton. *Journal of the Royal Central Asian Society*, vol. 30, part 2 (Jan. 1943), p. 142-58.

A study by a British political officer of the social organization of the tribes of the Western Aden Protectorate.

251 **Doctor among the bedouins.**
Eva Hoeck, translated from the German by Mervyn Savill. London: Robert Hale, 1962. 192p. map.

This work recounts the experiences of a woman doctor in the Yemen and in Ḥaḍramawt in the 1950s.

252 **The Arabian Peninsula: society and politics.**
Edited by Derek Hopwood. London: George Allen & Unwin, 1972. 320p. 2 maps. (School of Oriental and African Studies: Studies on Modern Asia and Africa, no. 8.)

A collection of papers on the Arabian Peninsula by several authors. The chapters relevant here are: 1, 'Some Western studies of Saudi Arabia, Yemen and Aden' by Derek Hopwood: and 12, 'Education and the press in South Arabia' by A. M. Luqman.

253 **Akhdam tribe in servitude.**
James Horgen. *Geographical magazine*, vol. 48, no. 9 (June 1976), p. 533-39.

A consideration of the negroid races of Tihāmah in the Yemen.

254 **A time in Arabia.**
Doreen Ingrams. London: John Murray, 1970. 154p. 2 maps.

An account of life in the Ḥaḍramawt by the wife of the British Resident Adviser.

255 **The Hadramaut in time of war.**
Harold Ingrams, Doreen Ingrams. *Geographical Journal*, vol. 105, nos. 1, 2 (Jan.-Feb. 1945), p. 1-29.

The authors describe Ḥaḍramawt during the Second World War.

256 **The Hadramaut: present and future.**
W. Harold Ingrams. *Geographical Journal*, vol. 92, no. 4 (Oct. 1938), p. 289-312.

A description of Ḥaḍramawt and the future prospects of the area.

257 **Changing veils: women and modernisation in north Yemen.**
Carla Makhlouf. London: Croom Helm, 1979. 103p. bibliog.

The author, an anthropologist, attempts to describe women's influence in Yemeni society and social change. Special attention is paid to the experiences of women in Ṣan'ā'.

258 **State policy and the position of women in South Yemen.**
Maxine D. Malyneux. *Peuples Méditerranéens*, vol. 12 (July-Sept. 1980), p. 33-49.

A study of the position of women in the People's Democratic Republic of Yemen based on interviews with senior members of the General Union of Yemeni Women.

Social Conditions and Organization

259 **Women's inheritance of land in highland Yemen.**
Martha Mundy. *Arabian Studies*, vol. 5 (1979), p. 161-87.

A study of the rights of inheritance of women due from the estates of their fathers in the Yemeni highlands.

260 **Women and development in Yemen Arab Republic.**
Cynthia Myntti. Eschborn, GFR: German Agency for Technical Co-operation, 1979. 106p.

The author examines the changing role and status of women in Yemeni society within the present social, economic and political atmosphere in the Yemen Arab Republic. She also analyses kinship and household organization, legal considerations, work roles, social roles, education and health. The conclusions reached are the result of a report made by a team of advisors to the Central Planning Organization in Yemen. The work also provides a summary and evaluation of current development programmes in Yemen.

261 **Das Qāt.** (Qat.)
Armin Schopen. Wiesbaden, GFR: Franz Steiner Verlag GMBH, 1978. 237p. map. bibliog. (Arbeiten aus dem Seminar für Völkkunde der Johann Wolfgang Goethe-Universität, Frankfurt am Main, Bd. 8).

A study of the history and cultivation of the plant *Catha edulis* Forskal in the Yemen Arab Republic. The plant is a mild narcotic and is habitually chewed by countless numbers of people in the Yemens. The author discusses the geography and climate of the Yemen Arab Republic, agriculture, irrigation and land ownership, the people and their religious and social groups. He also considers: *qāt*; its origin; cultivation; harvest; sale and use; *qāt* sessions and their significance and function; and its association with social events. The book ends with some original Arabic texts on the subject of *qāt*.

262 **The Ma'n 'gypsies' of the West Aden Protectorate.**
R. B. Serjeant. *Anthropos*, vol. 56 (1961), p. 737-49.

Anthropological notes on the Ma'n gypsies who were found in the Bayḥān and Dathīnah areas of South Arabia.

263 **The quarters of Tarīm and their tanṣūrahs.**
R. B. Serjeant. *Le Muséon,* vol. 63, no. 1-4 (1950), p. 277-84.

A study of the quarters of the Ḥaḍramawt town of Tarīm and the rallying-song of the quarters (sing. *tanṣūrah*).

264 **The Saiyids of Ḥaḍramawt.**
Robert Bertram Serjeant. London: School of Oriental and African Studies, 1957. 29p.

A scholarly discussion of the descendants of the Prophet in Ḥaḍramawt and their history and social standing within the community.

265 **South Arabian hunt.**
Robert Bertram Serjeant. London: Luzac, 1976. 143p. 2 maps.

A discussion of the traditional ritual ibex hunt in Southern Arabia, with additional material on the literary sources, hunting poems and hunting in Islamic law.

266 **The 'White Dune' at Abyan: an ancient place of pilgrimage in Southern Arabia.**
R. B. Serjeant. *Journal of Semitic Studies*, vol. 16, no. 1 (Spring 1971), p. 74-83.

The author discusses an ancient pilgrimage rite to the White Dune, a ridge of sand in the Abyan area of South Arabia.

267 **Socio-economic study of Hojjuriyya district, Yemen Arab Republic.**
Salah M. Yacoub, Akil Akil. Beirut: American University, 1971. 46p. map. (Faculty of Agricultural Sciences, no. 49.)

A socio-economic study of the Ḥujariyyah area of the Southern Yemen Arab Republic.

Arabian and Islamic studies.
See item no. 1.

Al-Yemen: a general social, political and economic survey.
See item no. 6.

An account of the British settlement of Aden in Arabia.
See item no. 7.

Survey of social and economic conditions in the Aden protectorate.
See item no. 8.

Yémen. (The Yemen).
See item no. 9.

City of Ṣan'ā'.
See item no. 10.

The Middle East and North Africa 1981-82.
See item no. 13.

Area handbook for the Yemens.
See item no. 16.

Ṣan'ā': an Arabian Islamic city.
See item no. 18.

Studies in Arabian history and civilisation.
See item no. 19.

Area handbook for the peripheral states of the Arabian Peninsula.
See item no. 20.

Social Conditions and Organization

The queen of Sheba's land: Yemen (Arabia Felix).
See item no. 21.

The Middle East: a physical, social and regional geography.
See item no. 26.

Inquiétant Yémen. (The disturbing Yemen).
See item no. 47.

Dutch travellers in Arabia in the seventeenth century. Parts I and II.
See item no. 48.

Some early travels in Arabia.
See item no. 50.

The kingdom of Melchior: adventure in south west Arabia.
See item no. 51.

The uneven road.
See item no. 52.

Southern Arabia.
See item no. 53.

Yemen on the threshold.
See item no. 54.

Travellers in Arabia.
See item no. 55.

Island of the dragon's blood.
See item no. 56.

The Oxford University expedition to Socotra.
See item no. 57.

Socotra: 'Island of Bliss'.
See item no. 58.

Arabia infelix or the Turks in Yamen.
See item no. 59.

Yémen 62-69: de la révolution 'sauvage' à la trève des guerriers. (The Yemen 62-69: from the 'savage' revolution to the warriors' truce).
See item no. 60.

A French doctor in the Yemen.
See item no. 61.

A French family in the Yemen.
See item no. 62.

A visit to the Idrisi territory in 'Asir and Yemen.
See item no. 63.

A journey through the Yemen and some general remarks upon that country.
See item no. 67.

Excursion into the Hajr province of Hadramaut.
See item no. 70.

Arabica.
See item no. 74.

The land of Uz.
See item no. 78.

El Yemen: tre anni nell' Arabia Felice. (Yemen: three years in Arabia Felix).
See item no. 79.

Travels through Arabia and other countries in the East.
See item no. 83.

Land and peoples of the Hadramaut, Aden protectorate.
See item no. 86.

San'a past and present.
See item no. 88.

The Yemen in 1937-38.
See item no. 91.

An exploration in the Hadramaut and journey to the coast.
See item no. 96.

Seen in the Hadhramaut.
See item no. 98.

The southern gates of Arabia.
See item no. 100.

A winter in Arabia.
See item no. 101.

A new journey in southern Arabia.
See item no. 102.

Travels in Arabia.
See item no. 104.

Kingship in ancient south Arabia.
See item no. 137.

Some features of social structure in Saba.
See item no. 140.

Temporary marriage in pre-Islamic south Arabia.
See item no. 142.

Social Conditions and Organization

Warfare in ancient south Arabia (2nd-3rd centuries A.D.).
See item no. 143.

Les hautes-terres du Nord-Yémen avant l'Islam. (The highlands of North Yemen before Islam).
See item no. 155.

Ḥaḍramawt.
See item no. 178.

Notes towards an understanding of the revolution in South Yemen.
See item no. 184.

Arab radical politics: al-Qawniyyūn al-'Arab and the Marxists in the turmoil of South Yemen, 1963-1967.
See item no. 208.

Fertility, mortality, migration and family planning in the Yemen Arab Republic.
See item no. 224.

People's Democratic Republic of Yemen: report on needs assessment for population assistance.
See item no. 225.

Les Yémens et leurs population. (The Yemens and their populations).
See item no. 226.

The Jews of Yemen.
See item no. 230.

Detroit's Yemeni workers.
See item no. 232.

Aspects of Labour migration from North Yemen.
See item no. 233.

Études sur les dialectes de l'Arabie méridionale. (Studies on the dialects of Southern Arabia).
See item no. 239.

The Zaydīs.
See item no. 242.

Amnesty International Briefing on People's Democratic Republic of Yemen.
See item no. 268.

Infant feeding in the Yemen Arab Republic.
See item no. 269.

The great health robbery: baby milk and medicines in Yemen.
See item no. 271.

Urban élites and colonialism: the nationalist élites of Aden and South Arabia.
See item no. 278.

Aden: évolution politique, économique et sociale de l'Arabie du Sud. (Aden: the political, economic and social evolution of South Arabia).
See item no. 280.

Yemen's unfinished revolution: socialism in the south.
See item no. 282.

Arab politics: the search for legitimacy.
See item no. 283.

Yemen: the search for a modern state.
See item no. 295.

Social structure and politics in the Yemen Arab Republic.
See item no. 300.

Socialist revolution in Arabia: a report from the People's Democratic Republic of Yemen.
See item no. 303.

A note on Law no. 1 of 1974 concerning the family, People's Democratic Republic of Yemen.
See item no. 310.

Yemen: political history, social structure and legal system.
See item no. 311.

Recent marriage legislation from al-Mukallā with notes on marriage customs.
See item no. 316.

Le sous-développement économique et social du Yémen: perspectives de la révolution Yémenite. (Economic and social underdevelopment in the Yemen: aspects of the Yemeni revolution).
See item no. 324.

Development potential and policies in the South Arabian countries: Yemen Arab Republic, People's Democratic Republic of Yemen, Sultanate of Oman.
See item no. 328.

People's Democratic Republic of Yemen: a review of economic and social development.
See item no. 329.

Some consequences of emigration for rural economic development in the Yemen Arab Republic.
See item no. 332.

Ḥajjah market.
See item no. 341.

Regular and permanent markets in the Ṣan'ā' region.
See item no. 342.

Guarding crops against *am-sibritāh* in north-west Yemen.
See item no. 350.

School leavers and job opportunities: a case study of short term shortages and long term surplus of school and university leavers in the Yemen Arab Republic 1975-1990.
See item no. 351.

The brain drain in the context of social change in Democratic Yemen and problems in high level manpower training at Aden University.
See item no. 352.

A fortified tower-house in Wādī Jirdān (Wāḥidī sultanate).
See item no. 357.

Architecture of the Islamic world; its history and social meaning.
See item no. 361.

Jewish domestic architecture in Ṣan'ā', Yemen.
See item no. 363.

The Islamic city.
See item no. 364.

Art of building in Yemen.
See item no. 365.

National science and technology policies in the Arab states.
See item no. 372.

Folklore and folk literature in Oman and Socotra.
See item no. 377.

The status of the Arab woman: a select bibliography.
See item no. 392.

A select bibliography of Yemen Arab Republic and People's Democratic Republic of Yemen.
See item no. 393.

The modern Arab woman: a bibliography.
See item no. 397.

Corpus des inscriptions et antiquités sud-arabes: bibliographie générale systématique. (A collection of writings about South Arabian inscriptions and antiquities: a general systematic bibliography).
See item no. 398.

Theses on Islam, the Middle East and North-west Africa 1880-1978.
See item no. 400.

Social Services, Health and Welfare

268 **Amnesty International Briefing on People's Democratic Republic of Yemen.**
Amnesty International. London: Amnesty International, 1976. 12p. map.

The contents of this report include: 'Number and analysis of prisoners and political context of imprisonment'; 'Legal situation'; 'Locality of detention centres'; 'Condition of detention'; 'Torture allegations'; 'Released prisoners'; 'Capital punishment'; and 'Disappearances'.

269 **Infant feeding in the Yemen Arab Republic.**
James Firebrace. London: Catholic Institute for International Relations, 1981. 20p.

An examination of the shift from breast feeding to bottle feeding and the role of the infant formula, milk powder and weaning food companies in this process.

270 **Ambition and reality: planning for health and basic health services in the Yemen Arab Republic.**
Jens Herrmann. Frankfurt, Berne, Las Vegas: Verlag Peter Lang, 1979. 135p. 4 maps. bibliog. (Medizin in Entwicklungsländern, no. 2.)

This book covers many aspects of health and health planning.

271 **The great health robbery: baby milk and medicines in Yemen.**
Dianna Melrose. Oxford: OXFAM, 1981. 50p. map.

A booklet describing social conditions in the Yemen Arab Republic and the political, economic and cultural factors which create obstacles to better health. Health services in the Yemen Arab Republic are also examined.

Western Arabia and the Red Sea.
See item no. 4.

Al-Yemen: a general social, political and economic survey.
See item no. 6.

Social Services, Health and Welfare

Survey of social and economic conditions in the Aden protectorate.
See item no. 8.

The Middle East: a political and economic survey.
See item no. 11.

Ṣan'ā': an Arabian Islamic city.
See item no. 18.

Who's who in the Arab world.
See item no. 23.

Yemen Arab Republic: a special report.
See item no. 24.

Yémen. (The Yemen).
See item no. 43.

A French doctor in the Yemen.
See item no. 61.

People's Democratic Republic of Yemen: report on needs assessment for population assistance.
See item no. 225.

Women's status and fertility in the Muslim world.
See item no. 243.

Some observations on Yemeni food habits.
See item no. 244.

Doctor among the bedouins.
See item no. 251.

Women and development in the Yemen Arab Republic.
See item no. 260.

People's Democratic Republic of Yemen: a review of economic and social development.
See item no. 329.

Emigration and economic development: the case of the Yemen Arab Republic.
See item no. 331.

Market opportunities and methods of doing business in the Yemen Arab Republic.
See item no. 337.

Ḥajjah market.
See item no. 341.

U.N. Statistical Yearbook.
See item no. 354.

National science and technology policies in the Arab states.
See item no. 372.

Folklore and folk literature in Oman and Socotra.
See item no. 377.

Folk-remedies from Ḥaḍramawt.
See item no. 378.

Politics

272 **The Free Yemeni Movement (1940-48) and its ideas on reform.**
A. Z. al-Abdin. *Middle Eastern Studies*, vol. 15 (Jan. 1979), p. 36-48.

A historical and political study of the Free Yemeni Movement.

273 **Aden and the Arab South.**
Nevill Barbour. *World Today*, vol. 15 (Jan.-Dec. 1959), p. 302-10.

The author considers the political problems of Aden and South Arabia in the 1950s.

274 **Army officers in Arab politics and society.**
Eliezer Be'eri. New York: Praeger; London: Pall Mall, 1969. 496p.

This work considers the influence of army officers in modern political events. It examines patterns of military coups, the motivation of Arab officer politicians and social processes in the contemporary Arab world. Chapter 10 looks at the influence of army officers in the Yemen between 1959 and 1967.

275 **South Arabia: violence and revolt.**
J. Bowyer Bell. *Conflict Studies*, no. 40 (Nov. 1973), p. 1-14.

A brief account of the Yemens from 1967-72. The article provides essential background material on the two countries and discusses: the National Front government in the People's Democratic Republic of Yemen, the economy of PDRY; the attempts to export revolution, notably to Oman; the republican government in the Yemen Arab Republic; tensions between the two countries; and prospects for the future.

276 **Soviet uses of proxies in the Third World: the case of Yemen.**
R. E. Bissell. *Soviet Studies*, vol. 30 (1978), p. 87-106.

A political study of Soviet-Yemen Arab Republic relations before and after the 1962 revolution.

277 **The Yemeni dilemma.**
William R. Brown. *Middle East Journal*, vol. 17, no. 4 (Autumn 1963), p. 349-67.

A study of the 1962 Yemen revolution, its background and the future prospects of the Republic.

278 **Urban élites and colonialism: the nationalist élites of Aden and South Arabia.**
A. S. Bujra. *Middle Eastern Studies*, vol. 6, no. 2 (May 1970), p. 189-212.

The author examines the emergence of nationalist élites and their relationship to political organizations.

279 **The emergence of Aden since 1956.**
A. P. Cumming-Bruce. *Royal Central Asian Journal*, vol. 49, nos. 3 and 4 (July-Oct. 1962), p. 307-16.

Reproduces an address to the Royal Central Asian Society in 1962 which described the political development of Aden from 1956.

280 **Aden: Évolution politique, économique et sociale de l'Arabie du Sud.** (Aden: the political, economic and social evolution of South Arabia.)
M. O. el Habashi. Algiers: Société nationale d'édition et de diffusion, 1966. 440p.

A consideration of the politics, economy and society of South Arabia.

281 **Revolutions and military rule in the Middle East: the Arab states; part II. Egypt, the Sudan, Yemen and Libya.**
George M. Haddad. New York: Robert Speller, 1973. 444p. bibliog.

Chapter 4 concerns the revolution and military rule of the Yemen Arab Republic after 1962.

282 **Yemen's unfinished revolution: socialism in the south.**
Fred Halliday. *Middle East Research and Information Project Reports,* vol. 9, no. 8, report no. 81 (Oct. 1979), p. 3-20.

A political, social and economic study of the People's Democratic Republic of Yemen. The author describes the country's record of progress, economic achievements and handicaps, the socio-political transformation of the nation, the Yemeni Socialist Party, the international arena and the crisis of June 1978.

283 **Arab politics: the search for legitimacy.**
Michael C. Hudson. New Haven, London: Yale University Press, 1977. 404p. map.

An analysis of recent political events. The work examines ruling structures, leaders, their ideologies, the background to social and cultural conditions, together with administrative processes. Chapter 9 contains a study of the politics of the Yemen Arab Republic and the People's Democratic Republic of Yemen.

284 **Arabia and the isles.**
Harold Ingrams. London: John Murray, 1966. 3rd edition. 400p. 2 maps.

An account of the author's personal experiences in the East African islands of Zanzibar and Pemba, as well as in Aden, Lahej and Ḥaḍramawt. The emphasis is on the author's own political role in these countries.

285 **Political development in the Hadhramaut.**
Harold Ingrams. *International Affairs,* vol. 21 (1945).

An account of the political development of the Eastern Aden Protectorate in the 1930s and 1940s.

286 **Peace in the Hadramaut.**
W. H. Ingrams. *Journal of the Royal Central Asian Society*, vol. 25 (Oct. 1938), p. 507-41.

The text of a lecture by the author on his famous 'Ingrams Peace' which was concerned with the pacification and disarming of the East Aden Protectorate.

287 **The problems of South-west Arabia.**
G. H. Jansen. *World Today*, vol. 19, no. 8 (August 1963), p. 337-43.

An examination of the political problems of South-west Arabia before independence.

288 **Hadramaut, Oman, Dhufar: the experience of revolution.**
J. B. Kelly. *Middle Eastern Studies*, vol. 12, no. 2 (May, 1976), p. 213-30.

A political study of revolution in both Ḥaḍramawt and in the Dhofar province of Oman.

289 **Coup and counter-coup in the Yaman 1948.**
Majid Khadduri. *International Affairs*, vol. 28 (Jan. 1952), p. 59-68.

A political study of the assassination in 1948 of Imam Yaḥyā and the eventual installation of Iman Aḥmad as ruler of the Yemen.

290 **Imperial outpost – Aden: its place in British strategic policy.**
Gillian King. London, New York, Toronto: Oxford University Press and the Royal Institute of International Affairs, 1964. 93p. 2 maps.

A discussion of British defence policy with particular reference to Aden and the Gulf. The work includes the following chapters: 4, 'Aden: the colony – the port and oil refinery, 1959 elections and the Aden TUC strike as a political weapon' (p. 42-5); 5, 'The Protectorate and the Federation of South Arabia – first steps towards federation, Aden's accession, the Yemeni coup and Aden's future, the Eastern Protectorate' (p. 57-73); and 6, 'Aden's neighbours – the Yemen' (p. 79-91).

291 **The problem of Aden.**
Gillian King. *The World Today*, vol. 18 (Jan.-Dec. 1962), p. 498-503.

Considers the political and constitutional problems of Aden.

292 **Middle East Contemporary Survey, 1976-77.**
Edited by Colin Legum. Tel Aviv: Shiloah Center for Middle Eastern and African Studies; New York, London: Holmes & Meier, 1978. 666p. 5 maps.

This work records and analyses political, economic, military and international developments in the Middle East. Part 1 deals with current issues; and part 2 contains a country by country review, including a survey of the People's Democratic Republic of Yemen (p. 549-64) and of the Yemen Arab Republic (p. 651-66). The subjects examined are power struggles, the sale of qāt, imports, budgets, armed forces statistics, and members of government, as well as relations with Saudi Arabia, Oman, the Palestine Liberation Organization, the Soviet Union and Cuba.

293 **Kuwayt and Aden: a contrast in British policies.**
Elizabeth Monroe. *Middle East Journal*, vol. 18, no. 1 (winter 1964), p. 63-74.

Discusses British government policies towards Kuwait and Aden.

294 **The Yemen Arab Republic and the politics of balance.**
J. E. Peterson. *Asian Affairs*, vol. 12 (1981), p. 254-66.

A political study of the Yemen Arab Republic.

Politics

295 **Yemen: the search for a modern state.**
J. E. Peterson. London, Canberra: Croom Helm, 1982. 221p. map. bibliog.

The book is concerned with political change in what is now the Yemen Arab Republic in the 20th century. The author concentrates on the differences between the imamate and the post-1962 republic. The volume includes chapters entitled: 1, 'Background to change in the Yemen Arab Republic' (p. 10-37); 2, 'Politics of the Imamate' (p. 37-68); 3, 'Process of political change' (p. 68-98); 4, 'Political dynamics of the Republic' (p. 98-136); 5, 'State-building and socio-economic development' (p. 136-70); and 6, 'Dilemmas of the 1980s' (p. 170-90).

296 **Aden and the Yemen.**
Bernard Reilly. London: HM Stationery Office, 1960. 67p. 4 maps.

Examines the Aden Protectorate and Aden Colony and their relations with the Yemen. The work includes: 1, 'Formation of the Aden Protectorate and conclusion of the Treaty of Sana with the Yemen' (p. 15-25); 2, 'Accession of Imam Ahmed and the Anglo-Yemeni conference of 1950' (p. 25-36); 3, 'Establishment of diplomatic relations with the Yemen and Yemeni interference in the Aden Protectorate' (p. 36-43); 5, 'Federation of the Aden Protectorate' (p. 52-63); and 6, 'Progress in Aden colony and the Aden Protectorate' (p. 63-68). Appendix 1 deals with the islands of Aden, Kamarān, Perim, Socotra, Kuria Muria Islands and appendix 2 has the text of the 1934 Treaty of Ṣan'ā'.

297 **Perilous politics in two Yemen states.**
R. B. Serjeant. *Geographical Magazine* (Aug. 1979), p. 767-74.

A consideration of the dangerous occupation of politicians in the Yemen Arab Republic and the People's Democratic Republic of Yemen.

298 **The Yemeni poet al-Zubayrī and his polemic against the Zaydī imams.**
R. B. Serjeant. *Arabian Studies*, vol. 5 (1979), p. 87-130.

A study of Muḥammad Maḥmūd al-Zubayrī's pamphlet, *The Imamate and its menace to Yemen unity*, written in the late 1950s.

299 **Political dictionary of the Middle East in the twentieth century.**
Yaacov Shimoni, Evyator Levine. New York: Quadrangle/New York Times Book Company, 1972. 510p.

Provides condensed information on the politics and peoples of the Middle East, and includes entries on South Arabia and Yemen.

300 **Social structure and politics in the Yemen Arab Republic.**
Robert W. Stookey. *Middle East Journal*, vol. 28, no. 3 (summer 1974), p. 248-61; vol. 28, no. 3 (autumn 1974), p. 409-19.

A consideration of the social and political background to the events in the Yemen, in particular the collapse of the 'Abd al-Raḥmān al-Iryānī government in 1974.

301 **South Yemen: a Marxist republic in Arabia.**
Robert W. Stookey. Boulder, Colorado: Westview Press; London: Croom Helm, 1982. 106p. 5 maps. bibliog. (Profiles: Nations of the Contemporary Middle East.)

A study designed for the general reader which examines the People's Democratic Republic of Yemen and includes a background historical survey.

302 **Yemen: the politics of the Yemen Arab Republic.**
Robert W. Stookey. Boulder, Colorado: Westview Press, 1978. 322p. 2 maps. bibliog. (Westview Special Studies on the Middle East.)

Despite the title, the author has attempted to produce a general political history of the Yemen from the earliest times to the present day. The chapter headings include: 'The ancient states'; 'The Islamic background'; 'The Fatimid states'; 'The Zaydī imamate'; 'The Rasulid state'; 'The Sharaf al-Dīn and Qāsimī dynasties'; 'The Mutawakkilite kingdom'; 'The revolution'; and 'Yemen reunited'.

303 **Socialist revolution in Arabia: a report from the People's Democratic Republic of Yemen.**
Joe Stork. *Middle East Research and Information Project Papers,* paper no. 15 (Feb. 1973), 1-25.

A detailed report on a visit to the People's Democratic Republic of Yemen. The author provides information, for example, on recent history, the building of the economy, the revolution, education, the courts and the position of women.

304 **The Middle East in revolution.**
Humphrey Trevelyan. London: MacMillan, 1970. 275p. map.

A personal record of three revolutions: Egypt in the 1950s; Iraq in the late 1950s and early 1960s; and the last days of British rule in Aden in 1967.

305 **Arab politics in the United Nations.**
Abdul Wahed Aziz Zindani. New Delhi: Caxton Press, 1977. 238p.

An expanded doctoral thesis on Arab policies and influence in the United Nations. Chapter VIII deals with the colony of Aden and the Protectorates prior to independence and chapter XI covers the civil war in Yemen up to the establishment of the Republic.

306 **Ingrams' peace in Hadhramaut.**
S. M. Zwemer. *Moslem World*, vol. 33, no. 2 (April 1943), p. 79-85.

A brief account of Ingrams' attempts to disarm the tribes of the Eastern Aden Protectorate in the 1940s and to implement peace.

Al-Yemen: a general social, political and economic survey.
See item no. 6.

An account of the British settlement of Aden in Arabia.
See item no. 7.

Yémen. (The Yemen).
See item no. 9.

The Middle East: a political and economic survey.
See item no. 11.

Middle East Annual Review.
See item no. 14.

Middle East Review.
See item no. 15.

Area handbook for the Yemens.
See item no. 16.

Area handbook for the peripheral states of the Arabian Peninsula.
See item no. 20.

The kingdom of Melchior: adventure in south west Arabia.
See item no. 51.

Perfumes of Araby: silhouettes of al-Yemen.
See item no. 73.

The war in the Yemen.
See item no. 76.

The land of Uz.
See item no. 78.

The Yemen in 1937-38.
See item no. 91.

Arabian assignment.
See item no. 93.

Tribes and tribulations: a journey in republican Yemen.
See item no. 94.

The Portuguese off the South Arabian Coast.
See item no. 173.

Notes towards an understanding of the revolution in South Yemen.
See item no. 184.

British naval operations against Turkish Yaman 1914-1919.
See item no. 185.

Imām Yaḥyā and the Yamanī uprising of 1911.
See item no. 187.

The political residents of Aden: biographical notes.
See item no. 191.

The Turkish attack on Aden 1915-1918.
See item no. 192.

The two Yemens.
See item no. 193.

British imperialism in southern Arabia.
See item no. 194.

Arabia: when Britain goes.
See item no. 195.

The Yemen revisited.
See item no. 196.

Aden under British rule: 1839-1967.
See item no. 197.

The conspirators.
See item no. 198.

Arabia without sultans.
See item no. 199.

The Yemen.
See item no. 201.

Aden.
See item no. 202.

The Yemen: imams, rulers and revolutions.
See item no. 204.

Kings of Arabia: the rise and set of the Turkish sovranty in the Arabian Peninsula (sic.).
See item no. 205.

The view from Steamer Point: being an account of three years in Aden.
See item no. 206.

Arab radical politics: al-Qawniyyūn al-'Arab and the Marxists in the turmoil of South Yemen, 1963-1967.
See item no. 208.

Politics

South Arabia: arena of conflict.
See item no. 211.

The war in the Yemen.
See item no. 213.

Last post: Aden 1964-1967.
See item no. 214.

Armies of the Middle East.
See item no. 215.

The Arabian Peninsula.
See item no. 216.

Yemen: the unknown war.
See item no. 217.

The two Yemens: historical perspectives and present attitudes.
See item no. 218.

Documents on the history of southwest Arabia: tribal warfare and foreign policy in Yemen, Aden and adjacent tribal kingdoms, 1920-29.
See item no. 219.

Notes on the Kathiri state of Hadhramaut.
See item no. 220.

Shades of Amber: a South Arabian episode.
See item no. 221.

Modern Yemen 1918-1966.
See item no. 223.

People's Democratic Republic of Yemen: report on needs assessment for population assistance.
See item no. 225.

Political conflict and stratification in Ḥaḍramaut.
See item no. 245.

The politics of stratification.
See item no. 246.

The social organisation of the tribes of the Aden Protectorate.
See item no. 250.

The Arabian Peninsula: society and politics.
See item no. 252.

State policy and the position of women in South Yemen.
See item no. 258.

Amnesty International Briefing on People's Democratic Republic of Yemen.
See item no. 268.

The great health robbery: baby milk and medicines in Yemen.
See item no. 271.

The Yemeni constitution and its religious orientation.
See item no. 307.

A constitution for South Arabia.
See item no. 308.

Aden and the Federation of South Arabia.
See item no. 309.

Yemen: political history, social structure and legal system.
See item no. 311.

Constitutions of the countries of the world: People's Democratic Republic of Yemen.
See item no. 313.

Constitutions of the countries of the world: Yemen Arab Republic.
See item no. 314.

Governments and politics of the Middle East in the twentieth century.
See item no. 317.

Yemen and the Western world.
See item no. 319.

Great Britain's relations with Yemen and Oman.
See item no. 320.

Labor relations and trades unions in Aden 1952-1960.
See item no. 353.

National science and technology policies in the Arab states.
See item no. 372.

Yemeni literature in Ḥajjah prisons, 1948-55.
See item no. 375.

The Arab press: news media and political process in the Arab world.
See item no. 381.

A select bibliography of Yemen Arab Republic and People's Democratic Republic of Yemen.
See item no. 393.

Law and Constitution

307 **The Yemeni constitution and its religious orientation.**
al-Tayib Zein al-Abdin. *Arabian Studies,* vol. 3 (1976), p. 115-25.

A study of the post-1962 republican constitution of the Yemen Arab Republic.

308 **A constitution for South Arabia.**
Gawain Bell. *Royal Central Asian Journal*, vol. 55, (Oct. 1966), p. 266-76.

Considers the problems of producing a constitution for the Federation of South Arabia.

309 **Aden and the Federation of South Arabia.**
J. Y. Brinton. Washington, DC: American Society of International Law, 1964. 81p.

A constitutional and legal examination of the Federal Government of South Arabia by an international lawyer.

310 **A note on Law no. 1 of 1974 concerning the family, People's Democratic Republic of Yemen.**
Isam Ghanem. *Arabian Studies*, vol. 3 (1976), p. 191-96.

A note on a law restricting polygamy by requiring the official permission of the court.

311 **Yemen: political history, social structure and legal system.**
Isam Ghanem. London: Arthur Probsthain, 1981. 25p. bibliog.

The author's main aim is to explain the legal system of the Yemen Arab Republic within the broader framework of the social and political developments of South-west Arabia.

312 **Notes on the development of Zaidi law.**
A. K. Kazi. *Abr-Nahrain*, vol. 2 (1960), p. 36-40.

A brief historical study of the development of Zaydī law.

313 **Constitutions of the countries of the world: People's Democratic Republic of Yemen.**
David W. McClintock. Dobbs Ferry, New York: Oceana Publications, 1971. 39p. bibliog.

Reproduces the text of the constitution of the People's Democratic Republic of Yemen with a chronology of recent events.

314 **Constitutions of the countries of the world: Yemen Arab Republic.**
David W. McClintock. Dobbs Ferry, New York: Oceana Publications, 1971. 27p. bibliog.

Reproduces the text of the Yemen Arab Republic's constitution and provides a chronology of recent events.

315 **The permanent constitution of the Yemen Arab Republic.**
Middle East Journal, vol. 25, no. 3 (summer 1971), p. 389-481.

Provides the text in English of the constitution of the Yemen Arab Republic.

316 **Recent marriage legislation from al-Mukallā with notes on marriage customs.**
R. B. Serjeant. *Bulletin of the School of Oriental and African Studies.* vol. 25, no. 3 (1962), p. 472-98.

The author provides a translation of a Quʻayṭī state marriage decree together with a commentary and some notes on Ḥaḍrami marriage customs.

Arabian and Islamic studies.
See item no. 1.

An account of the British settlement of Aden in Arabia.
See item no. 7.

Survey of social and economic conditions in the Aden protectorate.
See item no. 8.

Who's who in the Arab world.
See item no. 23.

Customary law documents as a source of history.
See item no. 172.

Women's inheritance of land in highland Yemen.
See item no. 259.

Women and development in Yemen Arab Republic.
See item no. 260.

South Arabian hunt.
See item no. 265.

Law and Constitution

Amnesty International Briefing on People's Democratic Republic of Yemen.
See item no. 268.

The Free Yemeni Movement (1940-48) and its ideas on reform.
See item no. 272.

The problem of Aden.
See item no. 291.

Socialist revolution in Arabia: a report from the People's Democratic Republic of Yemen.
See item no. 303.

The Arab business Yearbook.
See item no. 335.

Water rights and irrigation practices in Laḥj.
See item no. 345.

Yemen Arab Republic.
See item no. 346.

Some irrigation systems in Ḥadramawt.
See item no. 348.

A fortified tower-house in Wādī Jirdān (Wāḥidī sultanate).
See item no. 357.

The status of the Arab woman: a select bibliography.
See item no. 392.

The modern Arab woman: a bibliography.
See item no. 397.

Theses on Islam, the Middle East and North-west Africa 1880-1978.
See item no. 400.

The Near East (South-west Asia and North Africa): a bibliographic study.
See item no. 401.

Administration

317 **Governments and politics of the Middle East in the twentieth century.**
H. B. Sharabi. Princeton, Toronto, London, New York: D. Van Nostrand Company, 1962. 296p. map. (Van Nostrand Political Science Series.)

A summary and guide to the politics and the structure and functioning of governments in the Middle East. Chapters 18 and 19 concern the Yemen and South Arabia.

Western Arabia and the Red Sea.
See item no. 4.

Al-Yemen: a general social, political and economic survey.
See item no. 6.

An account of the British settlement of Aden in Arabia.
See item no. 7.

Area handbook for the Yemens.
See item no. 16.

Ṣan'ā': an Arabian Islamic city.
See item no. 18.

The queen of Sheba's land: Yemen (Arabia Felix).
See item no. 21.

Who's who in the Arab world.
See item no. 23.

Administrative division and land use in the Yemen Arab Republic.
See item no. 33.

Population distribution, administrative division and land use in the Yemen Arab Republic.
See item no. 34.

Democratic Yemen today.
See item no. 44.

Kingship in ancient south Arabia.
See item no. 137.

Administration

L'institution monarchique en Arabie méridionale avant l'Islam. (The institution of the monarchy in pre-Islamic South Arabia).
See item no. 156.

The Ayyubids and Rasulids: the transfer of power in the 7th/13th century Yemen.
See item no. 177.

Aden and the Federation of South Arabia.
See item no. 309.

Development potential and policies in the South Arabian countries: Yemen Arab Republic, People's Democratic Republic of Yemen, Sultanate of Oman.
See item no. 328.

Foreign Relations

318 **Resolution of the Yemen crisis, 1963: a case study in mediation.**
Christopher J. McMullen. Washington, DC: Institute for the Study of Diplomacy, School of Foreign Service, 1980. 51p.

A case study in US diplomacy after the 1962 revolution in Yemen.

319 **Yemen and the Western world.**
Eric Macro. London: C. Hurst, 1968. 150p. map. bibliog.

The author attempts to analyse the external relations of the Yemen since the time of the Portuguese, Dutch and French in the 15th century. Trade and politics, the frontier problem and Anglo-Yemeni relations are among the subjects discussed and an account of the two Yemens is provided down to the 1960s.

320 **Great Britain's relations with Yemen and Oman.**
Rupert May. *Middle Eastern Affairs*, vol. 11, no. 5 (May 1960), p. 142-49.

The author contrasts Anglo-Yemeni with Anglo-Omani relations in the 1950s.

321 **Conflict in the Yemens and superpower involvement.**
J. E. Peterson. Washington, DC: Center for Contemporary Arab Studies Georgetown University, 1981. 39p. map.

Examines the border conflict between the People's Democratic Republic of Yemen and the Yemen Arab Republic and the involvement of the United States and the Soviet Union.

The Middle East: a political and economic survey.
See item no. 11.

Area handbook for the peripheral states of the Arabian Peninsula.
See item no. 20.

Foreign interventions and occupations of Kamarān island.
See item no. 186.

The Turkish-Italian war in the Yemen 1911-1912.
See item no. 188.

Foreign Relations

Al-Yaman and the Turkish occupation 1849-1914.
See item no. 189.

The Yamani island of Kamarān during the Napoleonic wars.
See item no. 190.

The Turkish attack on Aden 1915-1918.
See item no. 192.

The Yemen: imams, rulers and revolutions.
See item no. 204.

Modern Yemen 1918-1966.
See item no. 223.

South Arabia: violence and revolt.
See item no. 275.

Soviet uses of proxies in the Third World: the case of Yemen.
See item no. 276.

Imperial outpost-Aden: its place in British strategic policy.
See item no. 290.

Middle East Contemporary Survey, 1976-77.
See item no. 292.

Kuwayt and Aden: a contrast in British policies.
See item no. 293.

Aden and the Yemen.
See item no. 296.

Economics

322 **The Arabia Peninsula: shaikhdoms and republics.**
London: Economist Intelligence Unit, 1978. quarterly.

A quarterly economic review, only one issue of which came out under this title, see *Bahrain, Qatar, Oman, the Yemens* (q.v.).

323 **Middle East Economies in the 1970s: a comparative approach.**
Hossein Askari, John Thomas Cummings. New York, Washington, London: Praeger Publishers, 1976. 581p. bibliog.

The sections of particular relevance are: the Yemen Arab Republic/North Yemen (education, planning, trade etc.); and the Yemen, People's Democratic Republic of/South Yemen (agriculture, fisheries, industry, land reform, planning and trade).

324 **Le sous-développement économique et social du Yémen: perspectives de la révolution Yémenite.** (Economic and social underdevelopment in the Yemen: aspects of the Yemeni revolution.)
Mohammed Said el Attar. Algiers: Tiers-Monde, 1964. 343p. map. bibliog.

An economic and social study of the post-revolution Yemen Arab Republic.

325 **Bahrain, Qatar, Oman, the Yemens.**
London: Economic Intelligence Unit, 2nd quarter, 1978- . quarterly.

A quarterly economic review. See also item no. 322 above.

326 **Development from below: local development associations in the Yemen Arab Republic.**
John M. Cohen, Mary Hébert, David B. Lewis, Jon C. Swanson. *World Development*, vol. 9, no. 11-12 (Nov.-Dec. 1981), p. 1039-61.

The authors examine economic development in the rural Yemen Arab Republic.

327 **Rural development in the Yemen Arab Republic: strategy issues in a capital surplus labour short economy.**
John M. Cohen, David B. Lewis. Cambridge, Massachusetts: Harvard Institute for International Development, 1979. 98p. 4 maps. bibliog. (Development Discussion Papers, no. 52.)

A study of the rural economy of the Yemen Arab Republic. The contents include: 'Paradigms and anomalies'; 'Rural development paradigms'; 'Rural economy of YAR'; 'Changing context in Yemen'; 'Yemen: a challenge to the paradigm'.

328 **Development potential and policies in the South Arabian countries: Yemen Arab Republic, People's Democratic Republic of Yemen, Sultanate of Oman.**
Michael Hofmann. Berlin, GFR: German Development Institute, 1982. 152p. 3 maps. bibliog.

A study of economic development and government policies in this field in the Yemen Arab Republic, the People's Democratic Republic of Yemen and Oman. Part 1 is an introduction, the Yemen Arab Republic is the subject of part 2, and the People's Democratic Republic of Yemen that of part 3. There are chapters on agriculture, industry, foreign aid and also on élites and government. The author provides innumerable statistics.

329 **People's Democratic Republic of Yemen: a review of economic and social development.**
International Bank for Reconstruction and Development. Washington, DC: World Bank, 1978. 169p. map. (World Bank Country Study).

An economic and social report based on the findings of a World Bank mission to the People's Democratic Republic of Yemen in 1978. The first part of the book is a survey including an assessment of macro-economic development of sector development and social development. The report deals with agriculture, fisheries, income distribution, employment, food, health, the oil industry, education, emigration, manufacture, material resources, transport and housing. The second part is a detailed statistical appendix.

330 **Economic changes in Yemen, Aden and Dhofar.**
Alexander Melamid. *Middle Eastern Affairs,* vol. 5, no. 3 (March 1954), p. 88-91.

Discusses the repercussions felt in the Yemen, Aden and Dhofar of the substantial oil revenues of the Gulf States. Other important products, coffee, minerals etc. are also touched upon.

331 **Emigration and economic development: the case of the Yemen Arab Republic.**
Jon C. Swanson. Boulder, Colorado: Westview Press, 1979. 108p. bibliog.

The author deals with the geography, climate and recent history of the area, subsistence agriculture, nutrition and cash cropping and emigration and its consequences.

332 **Some consequences of emigration for rural economic development in the Yemen Arab Republic.**
J. C. Swanson. *Middle East Journal*, vol. 33 (1979), p. 34-43.

A study of the effects of emigration from rural areas of the Yemen Arab Republic.

333 **The Middle East in the coming decade.**
John Waterbury, Raqaei el Mallakh. New York: McGraw-Hill, 1978. 219p. bibliog.

A study of the economic prospects for the Middle East during the 1980s. Of particular relevance are the sections on Yemen, North and Yemen, South.

Arabian and Islamic studies.
See item no. 1.

Western Arabia and the Red Sea.
See item no. 4.

Al-Yemen: a general social, political and economic survey.
See item no. 6.

The Middle East: a political and economic survey.
See item no. 11.

The Middle East and North Africa 1981-82.
See item no. 13.

Middle East Annual Review.
See item no. 14.

Middle East Review.
See item no. 15.

Area handbook for the Yemens.
See item no. 16.

Area handbook for the peripheral states of the Arabian Peninsula.
See item no. 20.

Who's who in the Arab world.
See item no. 23.

Economics

Yemen Arab Republic: a special report.
See item no. 24.

Yémen. (The Yemen).
See item no. 43.

Democratic Yemen today.
See item no. 44.

Inquiétant Yémen. (The disturbing Yemen).
See item no. 47.

Archaeological discoveries in south Arabia.
See item no. 109.

The diary of a Mocha coffee agent.
See item no. 165.

The Portuguese off the South Arabian Coast.
See item no. 173.

Notes on the Kathiri state of Hadhramaut.
See item no. 220.

Democratic Yemen.
See item no. 228.

Yemen.
See item no. 229.

The Jews of Yemen.
See item no. 230.

Detroit's Yemeni workers.
See item no. 232.

Some observations on Yemeni food habits.
See item no. 244

Sozio-ökonomische Aspekt der Stammesdemokratie in Nordost-Yemen.
(Socio-economic aspects of tribal democracy in north-east Yemen.)
See item no. 248.

Women and development in the Yemen Arab Republic.
See item no. 260.

Socio-economic study of Hojjuriyya district, Yemen Arab Republic.
See item no. 267.

The great health robbery: baby milk and medicines in Yemen.
See item no. 271.

South Arabia: violence and revolt.
See item no. 275.

Aden: évolution politique, économique et sociale de l'Arabie du Sud.
(Aden: the political, economic and social evolution of South Arabia).
See item no. 280.

Yemen's unfinished revolution: socialism in the south.
See item no. 282.

Middle East Contemporary Survey, 1976-77.
See item no. 292.

Yemen: the search for a modern state.
See item no. 295.

Socialist revolution in Arabia: a report from the People's Democratic Republic of Yemen.
See item no. 303.

The Arabia Peninsula: shaikhdoms and republics.
See item no. 322.

The Arabs' new frontier.
See item no. 334.

The Arab business Yearbook.
See item no. 335.

Major companies of the Arab world.
See item no. 336.

Market opportunities and methods of doing business in the Yemen Arab Republic.
See item no. 337.

A market consultancy report to the Land Resources Division, Ministry of Overseas Development, on the Montane Plains/Wadi Rima Project, Yemen Arab Republic.
See item no. 343.

Yemen Arab Republic.
See item no. 346.

Yemeni agriculture and economic change.
See item no. 349.

The brain drain in the context of social change in Democratic Yeman and problems in high level manpower training at Aden University.
See item no. 352.

Technology transfer and change in the Arab world.
See item no. 374.

A select bibliography of Yemen Arab Republic and People's Democratic Republic of Yemen.
See item no. 393.

Theses on Islam, the Middle East and North-west Africa 1880-1978.
See item no. 400.

The Near East (South-west Asia and North Africa): a bibliographic study.
See item no. 401.

Finance and Banking

334 **The Arabs' new frontier.**
Robert Stephens. London. Temple Smith, 1973. 256p.

A general study of the first ten years of the operation of the Kuwait Fund for Arab Economic Development. Chapter 14, p. 218-43, concerns both Yemens.

Survey of social and economic conditions in the Aden protectorate.
See item no. 8.

The Middle East: a political and economic survey.
See item no. 11.

Middle East Annual Review.
See item no. 14.

Middle East Review.
See item no. 15.

Who's who in the Arab world.
See item no. 23.

The Arab business Yearbook.
See item no. 335.

Major companies of the Arab world.
See item no. 336.

Cultural policy in the Yemen Arab Republic.
See item no. 367.

Science and science policy in the Arab world.
See item no. 373.

The Developing Areas: a classed bibliography of the Joint Bank-Fund Library, World Bank Group & International Monetary Fund, Washington DC. 3 vols. vol. 2 Africa and the Middle East.
See item no. 387.

Trade and Industry

335 **The Arab Business Yearbook.**
Compiled by Giselle Bricault, Michael Donovan. London: Graham & Trotman, 1976. 579p.

This volume contains economic, financial and banking information for the whole of the Arab world including the Yemens. The work includes currency conversion charts and covers: taxation; customs; tariffs; trade and foreign investment regulations; and provides addresses and other information useful to the business traveller.

336 **Major companies of the Arab world.**
Editorial manager Giselle C. Bricault. London: Graham & Trotman, 1977. 559p.

A list of companies, country by country, in the Arab world. See in particular Yemen (Arab Republic) p. 535-49 and Yemen (People's Democratic Republic) p. 549-57.

337 **Market opportunities and methods of doing business in the Yemen Arab Republic.**
Committee for Middle East Trade. London: Committee for Middle East Trade, 1978. 115p. map.

The contents include: 'Economy'; 'Agriculture'; 'Industry'; 'Services (education, health etc.)'; 'Opportunities for British exporters'; 'Foreign investment'; and 'Communications'.

338 **Historie du commerce entre le Levant et l'Europe.** (The history of trade between Europe and the East.)
G. B. Depping. New York: Burt Franklin, 1970. reprint. 2 vols.

A history of trade between Europe and the East from the time of the Crusades to the founding of the American colonies. The first chapter of vol. 1 deals very briefly with early trade through Aden.

339 **Islam and the trade of Asia: a colloquium.**
D. S. Richards. Oxford, England: Bruno Cassirer, 1970. 267p.

Reproduces the papers delivered at the Second International Colloquium of the Near Eastern History group which was held in Oxford in 1967. The papers include details of: trade in Yemen and Ḥaḍramawt in early Islamic and mediaeval times; commercial techniques; and South Arabian trade with East Africa and the East.

340 **Asia.**
Edited by Sigfred Taubert, Peter Wiedhaas. Munich, GFR; New York, London, Paris: K. G. Saur, 1981. 284p. maps. (Book Trade of the World.)

This general reference book on the book trade throughout Asia includes two brief pages on the Yemen Arab Republic and the People's Democratic Republic of Yemen. Both entries include only two sections: general information including area, population, major towns, religion, language, and currency; and sources of information.

341 **Ḥajjah market.**
Robert Wilson. *Arabian Studies,* vol. 2 (1975), p. 204-10.

Some notes on the market of Ḥajjah in Northwest Yemen. The article contains a plan of the market and some photographs.

342 **Regular and permanent markets in the Ṣan'ā' region.**
Robert Wilson. *Arabian Studies*, vol. 5 (1979), p. 189-91.

A brief note on the markets in the area north of Ṣan'ā'.

An account of the British settlement of Aden in Arabia.
See item no. 7.

Survey of social and economic conditions in the Aden protectorate.
See item no. 8.

City of Ṣan'ā'.
See item no. 10.

The Middle East: a political and economic survey.
See item no. 11.

Ṣan'ā': an Arabian Islamic city.
See item no. 18.

The queen of Sheba's land: Yemen (Arabia Felix).
See item no. 21.

Who's who in the Arab world.
See item no. 23.

Trade and Industry

Arabia infelix or the Turks in Yamen.
See item no. 59.

From Cana (Husn Ghorab) to Sabbatha (Shabwa): the South Arabian incense road.
See item no. 71.

Archaeological discoveries in south Arabia.
See item no. 109.

Histoire de Thamoud. (History of Thamud).
See item no. 144.

Arabian frankincense in antiquity according to classical sources.
See item no. 151.

The diary of a Mocha coffee agent.
See item no. 165.

The Portuguese off the South Arabian Coast.
See item no. 173.

The history of Aden.
See item no. 209.

Detroit's Yemeni workers.
See item no. 232.

Aspects of labour migration from North Yemen.
See item no. 233.

Middle East Contemporary Survey, 1976-77.
See item no. 292.

Yemen and the Western world.
See item no. 319.

Middle East Economies in the 1970s: a comparative approach.
See item no. 323.

Development potential and policies in the South Arabian countries: Yemen Arab Republic, People's Democratic Republic of Yemen, Sultanate of Oman.
See item no. 328.

People's Democratic Republic of Yemen: a review of economic and social development.
See item no. 329.

Economic changes in Yemen, Aden and Dhofar.
See item no. 330.

Major companies of the Arab world.
See item no. 336.

Market opportunities and methods of doing business in the Yemen Arab Republic.
See item no. 337.

Labor relations and trades unions in Aden 1952-1960.
See item no. 353.

U.N. Statistical Yearbook.
See item no. 354.

National science and technology policies in the Arab states.
See item no. 372.

Agriculture, Irrigation and Fisheries

343 **A market consultancy report to the Land Resources Division, Ministry of Overseas Development, on the Montane Plains/Wadi Rima Project, Yemen Arab Republic.**
P. J. Boustead. London: Tropical Products Institute, Ministry of Overseas Development, 1974. 38p.

A report on the Wadi Rima' agricultural project. The headings include: 'Crop production and marketing in the project area'; 'Prospects for crop production and marketing'; 'Conclusions and recommendations'.

344 **The possible origin of the dwarf cattle of Socotra.**
M. D. Gwynne. *Geographical Journal*, vol. 133 (1967), p. 39-42.

A semi-technical study of the dwarf cattle of Socotra and their origin.

345 **Water rights and irrigation practices in Laḥj.**
A. M. A. Maktari. Cambridge, England: Cambridge University Press, 1971. 174p. 2 maps. bibliog. (University of Cambridge Oriental Publications, no. 21.)

This is a study of the application of customary and Islamic law in the area of Lahej, an area a little north of Aden, as far as it concerns water rights and irrigation. The fieldwork was carried out by the author in the late 1960s.

346 **Yemen Arab Republic.**
Compiled by P. M. Reilly. Surbiton, England: Land Resources Division, Ministry of Overseas Development, 1978. 87p. (Land Resources Bibliography, no. 11.)

A bibliography of land resources under the following headings: 'Agriculture'; 'Animal science'; 'Botany'; 'Climatology'; 'Crops'; 'Cultural studies'; 'Economics'; 'Forestry'; 'Geoscience'; 'Land tenure'; 'Maps'; 'Natural resources'; 'Population'; 'Soil science'; and 'Water resources'.

347 **The cultivation of cereals in medieval Yemen.**
Robert Bertram Serjeant. *Arabian Studies*, vol. 1 (1974), p. 25-74.

The translation of a 14th-century Arabic treatise on cereal cultivation in the Yemen.

348 **Some irrigation systems in Ḥaḍramawt.**
R. B. Serjeant. *Bulletin of the School of Oriental and African Studies*, vol. 27, part 1 (1964), p. 33-76.

A study of irrigation in the Ḥaḍramawt based on legal texts and the author's own fieldwork. The article contains black and white photographs and some line drawings.

349 **Yemeni agriculture and economic change.**
Richard Tutwiler, Shella Carapico. Ṣan'ā', Yemen Arab Republic American Institute for Yemeni Studies, 1981. 191p. 5 maps. bibliog. (American Institute for Yemeni Studies Series, no. 1.)

A study of traditional highlands' agriculture with specific reference to farm production and marketing patterns in the Ibb and 'Amrān areas.

350 **Guarding crops against *am-sibrītah* in north-west Yemen.**
Robert Wilson. *Arabian Studies*, vol. 4 (1978), p. 209-10.

Brief notes on guarding the sorghum and bean crops in Yemen against the porcupine.

Arabian and Islamic studies.
See item no. 1.

Western Arabia and the Red Sea.
See item no. 4.

An account of the British settlement of Aden in Arabia.
See item no. 7.

Survey of social and economic conditions in the Aden protectorate.
See item no. 8.

The Middle East: a political and economic survey.
See item no. 11.

Arabian Studies.
See item no. 17.

Ṣan'ā': an Arabian Islamic city.
See item no. 18.

Yemen Arab Republic: a special report.
See item no. 24.

Democratic Yemen today.
See item no. 44.

Socotra: 'Island of Bliss'.
See item no. 58.

Arabia infelix or the Turks in Yamen.
See item no. 59.

The land of Uz.
See item no. 78.

Archaeological discoveries in south Arabia.
See item no. 109.

The diary of a Mocha coffee agent.
See item no. 165.

Some observations on Yemeni food habits.
See item no. 244.

Das Qãt. (Qat).
See item no. 261.

Middle East Economies in the 1970s: a comparative approach.
See item no. 323.

Development from below: local development associations in the Yemen Arab Republic.
See item no. 326.

Rural development in the Yemen Arab Republic: strategy issues in a capital surplus labour short economy.
See item no. 327.

Development potential and policies in the South Arabian countries: Yemen Arab Republic, People's Democratic Republic of Yemen, Sultanate of Oman.
See item no. 328.

People's Democratic Republic of Yemen: a review of economic and social development.
See item no. 329.

Economic changes in Yemen, Aden and Dhofar.
See item no. 330.

Emigration and economic development: the case of the Yemen Arab Republic.
See item no. 331.

Some consequences of emigration for rural economic development in the Yemen Arab Republic.
See item no. 332.

Market opportunities and methods of doing business in the Yemen Arab Republic.
See item no. 337.

Ḥajjah market.
See item no. 341.

U.N. Statistical Yearbook.
See item no. 354.

National science and technology policies in the Arab States.
See item no. 372.

Theses on Islam, the Middle East and North-west Africa 1880-1978.
See item no. 400.

Employment and Manpower

351 **School leavers and job opportunities: a case study of short term shortages and long term surplus of school and university leavers in the Yemen Arab Republic 1975-1990.**
Clive Sinclair, James Locknat. Geneva: International Labour Office, 1977. 26p. (World Employment Programme Research, Working papers, no. 17.)

A study of job opportunities for school and university leavers in the Yemen Arab Republic.

352 **The brain drain in the context of social change to Democratic Yemen and problems in high level manpower training at Aden University.**
Mohamed Gaffar Zain. In: *Arab brain drain: proceedings of UN Seminar, Beirut* 1980. Edited by A. B. Zahlan. London: Ithaca, 1981. p. 43-58.

A study of the social and economic aspects of the brain drain from the People's Democratic Republic of Yemen.

Ṣan'ā': an Arabian Islamic city.
See item no. 18.

Aspects of labour migration from North Yemen.
See item no. 233.

Rural development in the Yemen Arab Republic: strategy issues in a capital surplus labour short economy.
See item no. 327.

People's Democratic Republic of Yemen: a review of economic and social development.
See item no. 329.

Emigration and economic development: the case of the Yemen Arab Republic.
See item no. 331.

Some consequences of emigration for rural economic development in the Yemen Arab Republic.
See item no. 332.

Labour and Trades Unions

353 **Labor relations and trades unions in Aden 1952-1960.**
D. C. Watt. *Middle East Journal*, vol. 16 (1962), p. 443-56.
An historical and political study of the Aden trades union movement in the 1950s.

Yemen Arab Republic: a special report.
See item no. 24.

Fertility, mortality, migration and family planning in the Yemen Arab Republic.
See item no. 224.

Aspects of labour migration from North Yemen.
See item no. 233.

Women and development in Yemen Arab Republic.
See item no. 260.

Rural development in the Yemen Arab Republic: strategy issues in a capital surplus labour short economy.
See item no. 327.

Statistics

354 **U.N. Statistical Yearbook.**
New York: United Nations, 1948- . annual.

Provides an up-to-date compendium of economic and social statistics for many countries of the world, including the Yemens. The topics covered include population, health, education, agriculture, fishing, energy, petroleum, trade and transport.

The Middle East and North Africa 1981-82.
See item no. 13.

Fertility, mortality, migration and family planning in the Yemen Arab Republic.
See item no. 224.

Democratic Yemen.
See item no. 228.

Yemen.
See item no. 229.

Middle East Contemporary Survey, 1976-77.
See item no. 292.

Development potential and policies in the South Arabian countries: Yemen Arab Republic, People's Democratic Republic of Yemen, Sultanate of Oman.
See item no. 328.

People's Democratic Republic of Yemen: a review of economic and social development.
See item no. 329.

The Arab business Yearbook.
See item no. 335.

Science and science policy in the Arab world.
See item no. 373.

Architecture and Planning

355 **North Yemen: images of the built environment.**
Centre for Middle Eastern and Islamic Studies, University of Durham. Durham: Centre for Middle Eastern and Islamic Studies, 1982. 20p.

A catalogue of an exhibition of colour photographs by Naomi Gazzard, held in Trevelyan College, Durham, May-June 1982.

356 **Yemen, land of builders.**
Paolo Costa, Ennio Vicario. Translated from the Italian by Daphne Newton. London: Academy Editions, 1978. 173p. map. bibliog.

A lavishly illustrated introduction to the architecture of the Yemen Arab Republic. Translated from the original *Yemen, paese di costruttori.*

357 **A fortified tower-house in Wādī Jirdān (Wāḥidī sultanate).**
B. Doe, R. B. Serjeant. *Bulletin of the School of Oriental and African Studies,* vol. 38, nos. 1 and 2 (1975), p. 1-23, 276-95.

A comprehensive study of the architecture of a tower-house in South Arabia, with illustrations and plans. The authors provide a glossary of technical architectural terms, and notes on such subjects as building and house law, builders, tools and materials.

358 **House building in the Hadramaut.**
W. H. Ingrams. *Geographical Journal*, vol. 85 (Jan.-June 1935), p. 370-72.

A brief study of house building in Ḥaḍramawt with photographs.

359 **Three medieval mosques in the Yemen.**
Ronald Lewcock, Gerald Rex Smith. *Oriental Art*, vol. 20 (1974), p. 75-86, 192-203.

A study, with photographs and line drawings, of three Rasulid mosques in Ta'izz. The headings include: 'Historical background'; 'Jāmi' al-Muẓaffar and its architectural origins'; 'The inscriptions'; 'The Ashrafiyyah and its architectural origins'; 'The Mu'tabiyyah and its architecture'; and 'Architectural origins'.

360 **Two early mosques in the Yemen: a preliminary report.**
Ronald Lewcock, Gerald Rex Smith. *Art and Architectural Research Papers,* vol. 4 (1973), p. 117-30.

A preliminary report, with illustrations, of the mosques of Shibām Kawkabān and Dhū Jiblah. The headings in this article include: 'The Shibām *Jāmi'* and its architecture'; 'Architectural origins'; 'The inscriptions'; 'The Dhū Jiblah *Jāmi'* and its architectural origins'; and 'The inscriptions'.

361 **Architecture of the Islamic world: its history and social meaning.**
Edited by George Michell. London: Thames & Hudson, 1978. 288p. map. bibliog.

A study of Islamic architecture in its cultural setting. The contents include: 'Key monuments of Islamic art: Arabia' by Geoffrey King and Ronald Lewcock in which the Great Mosque of Ṣan'ā', the Bakiriyyah mosque in Ṣan'ā', the Ashrafiyyah mosque in Ta'izz and the mosque of Shibām, Ḥaḍramawt, People's Democratic Republic of Yemen, are briefly described.

362 **Conservation in Yemen.**
Venetia Porter. *The Arab Cultural Scene* (1982), p. 132-34.

A brief review of the problems of the conservation of historic buildings in the Yemen Arab Republic.

363 **Jewish domestic architecture in Ṣan'ā', Yemen.**
Carl Rathjens, with an introduction and an appendix on seventeenth century documents relating to Jewish houses in Ṣan'ā' by S. D. Goitein. Jerusalem: Israel Oriental Society, 1957. 80p. map. illus.

A study, with photographs and line drawings of Jewish domestic architecture in Ṣan'ā'.

364 **The Islamic city.**
Edited by R. B. Serjeant. Paris: UNESCO, 1980. 210p.

Contains the papers delivered at a colloquium held in the Middle East Centre, Cambridge University, in July, 1976. The papers included: 'Social stratification in Arabia' by R. B. Serjeant and 'Ṣan'ā'' by Paolo M. Costa.

365 **Art of building in Yemen.**
Fernando Varanda. London: Art and Archaeology Research Papers, 1981. 292p. 4 maps. illus.

A lavishly illustrated book on the domestic architecture of the Yemen Arab Republic.

Architecture and Planning

366 **Ṣan'ā': a report to Unesco.**
Michael Welbank, Julio Figueiras. London: Shankland & Cox Partnership, 1978. 72p. 15 maps. illus.

A report on the planning and architecture of Ṣan'ā' under the headings: 'Planning framework'; 'Environmental improvements'; 'Conservation'; and 'Programme'. Includes black and white illustrations.

Arabian and Islamic studies.
See item no. 1.

An account of the British settlement of Aden in Arabia.
See item no. 7.

City of Ṣan'ā'.
See item no. 10.

Arabian Studies.
See item no. 17.

'Ṣan'ā': an Arabian Islamic city.
See item no. 18.

Yemen Arab Republic: a special report.
See item no. 24.

Archäologische Berichte aus dem Jemen. (Archaeological reports from the Yemen).
See item no. 113.

An archaeological journey to Yemen.
See item no. 119.

The antiquities of South Arabia.
See item no. 146.

'Adan.
See item no. 168.

Women and development in Yemen Arab Republic.
See item no. 260.

Middle East Economies in the 1970s: a comparative approach.
See item no. 323.

Science and science policy in the Arab world.
See item no. 373.

Education and Culture

367 **Cultural policy in the Yemen Arab Republic.**
Abdul-Rahman Al-Hadda. Paris: UNESCO, 1982. 74p.

A study of the cultural policies of the government of the Yemen Arab Republic which includes chapters concerning: the role of culture in national liberation; the organizational and financial structure of cultural institutions; Yemeni culture and international co-operation; planning and cultural development; the development of cultural media; the development of schools; popular arts; and antiquities and museums.

368 **Education in the Hadhramaut.**
Harold Ingrams. *Overseas Education*, vol. 16, no. 4 (July, 1945), p. 145-51.

The history of the education department and of education in the Ḥaḍramawt coastal region in the east of the People's Democratic Republic of Yemen.

369 **Education and the press in South Arabia.**
Ali Muhammad Luqman. In: *The Arabian Peninsula: society and politics* (q.v.). Edited by Derek Hopwood. London: George Allen & Unwin, 1972, p. 255-71.

This is chapter 12 of the book. The author divides the chapter into two separate parts: education and the press. In the first part he provides the historical background to both Aden and the Protectorates, and other topics which are covered include technical education, teacher training, post-secondary education and the future of education. In the second part he briefly sketches the history of the press in Aden before surveying the post-independence press.

370 **Islamic education: its traditions and modernization into the Arab National Systems.**
A. L. Tibawi. London: Luzac & Company, 1972. 226p.

The study falls into three main parts: part 1 is a history of Islamic education, and its theory and practice from the rise of Islam to the dawn of the 19th century; part 2 traces the development of the education system in Yemen and South Yemen, Iraq, Jordan, Palestine, Egypt, the Sudan, Lebanon, Syria, Libya, Tunisia, Algeria, Morocco, Saudi Arabia and Kuwait; and part 3 is an interpretive review of purely educational and general cultural problems of common interest to the fourteen systems studied in part 2.

Education and Culture

An account of the British settlement of Aden in Arabia.
See item no. 7.

Survey of social and economic conditions in the Aden protectorate.
See item no. 8.

The Middle East: a political and economic survey.
See item no. 11.

The queen of Sheba's land: Yemen (Arabia Felix).
See item no. 21.

Who's who in the Arab world.
See item no. 23.

Yemen Arab Republic: a special report.
See item no. 24.

Yémen. (The Yemen).
See item no. 43.

People's Democratic Republic of Yemen: report on needs assessment for population assistance.
See item no. 225.

The Arabian Peninsula: society and politics.
See item no. 252.

Women and development in the Yemen Arab Republic.
See item no. 260.

The great health robbery: baby milk and medicines in Yemen.
See item no. 271.

Socialist revolution in Arabia: a report from the People's Democratic Republic of Yemen.
See item no. 303.

Middle East Economies in the 1970s: a comparative approach.
See item no. 323.

People's Democratic Republic of Yemen: a review of economic and social development.
See item no. 329.

Market opportunities and methods of doing business in the Yemen Arab Republic.
See item no. 337.

School leavers and job opportunities: a case study of short term shortages and long term surplus of school and university leavers in the Yemen Arab Republic 1975-1990.
See item no. 351.

The brain drain in the context of social change in Democratic Yemen and problems in high level manpower training at Aden University.
See item no. 352.

U.N. Statistical Yearbook.
See item no. 354.

National science and technology policies in the Arab states.
See item no. 372.

Science and science policy in the Arab world.
See item no. 373.

A book world directory of the Arab countries, Turkey and Iran.
See item no. 384.

The status of the Arab woman: a select bibliography.
See item no. 392.

Arab education 1956-1978: a bibliography.
See item no. 394.

The Near East (South-west Asia and North Africa): a bibliographic study.
See item no, 401.

Science and Technology

371 **Mathematical astronomy in medieval Yemen.**
David A. King. *Arabian Studies,* vol. 5 (1979), p. 61-65.

A brief study of astronomical writings in the Yemen from the 9th to the 15th century.

372 **National science and technology policies in the Arab states.**
UNESCO. Paris: UNESCO, 1976. 214p. bibliog.

Provides information concerning the science and technology policies of the Arab member states. See in particular: the Yemen Arab Republic, p. 205-11; and the People's Democratic Republic of Yemen, p. 211-14. The subjects covered include: geopolitical setting; capital and population; natural resources; political structure; socio-economic indicators; educational indicators; socio-economic planning; agriculture; fisheries; industry; energy; education; and health.

373 **Science and science policy in the Arab world.**
A. B. Zahlan. London: Croom Helm, 1980. 205p.

An attempt to assess trends in scientific policy and development. The study highlights the need for high professional standards and sound institutions in order to institute long-term planning and scientific research. It includes statistics concerning scientific manpower, the funding of research, financial resources, and policy making bodies throughout the Middle East, including the Yemen Arab Republic and the People's Democratic Republic of Yemen.

374 **Technology transfer and change in the Arab world.**
Edited by A. B. Zahlan. Oxford: Pergamon Press (for the United Nations), 1978. 506p. bibliog.

The proceedings of a seminar of the United Nations Economic Commission for Western Asia organized by the Natural Resources, Science and Technology Division, Beirut, 1977. See in particular the sections dealing with the Yemen Arab Republic and the People's Democratic Republic of Yemen.

Yemen Arab Republic.
See item no. 346.

A fortified tower-house in Wādī Jirdān (Wāḥidī sultanate).
See item no. 357.

The Near East (South-west Asia and North Africa): a bibliographic study.
See item no. 401.

Literature

375 **Yemeni literature in Ḥajjah prisons, 1948-55.**
Aḥmad Muḥammad al-Shāmī. *Arabian Studies*, vol. 2 (1975), p. 43-60.

An account of the literary school which sprang up among those imprisoned in Ḥajjah in northwest Yemen by Imam Yaḥyā after the unsuccessful coup d'état of 1948. The author was himself imprisoned and describes these literary activities from personal experience.

Arabian Studies.
See item no. 17.

Études sur les dialectes de l'Arabie méridionale. (Studies on the dialects of Southern Arabia).
See item no. 239.

South Arabian hunt.
See item no. 265.

The Yemeni poet al-Zubayrī and his polemic against the Zaydī imams.
See item no. 298.

Theses on Islam, the Middle East and North-west Africa 1880-1978.
See item no. 400.

The Near East (South-west Asia and North Africa): a bibliographic study.
See item no. 401.

Visual Arts

376 **South Arabian gold jewellery.**
Geoffrey Turner. *Iraq*, vol. 1, part 2 (autumn 1973), p. 127-41.
A catalogue of some forty five items of pre-Islamic jewellery from the Muncherjee Collection in the Aden Museum. The author provides descriptions of each item and the article is accompanied by line drawings.

Ṣan'ā': an Arabian Islamic city.
See item no. 18.

The pre-Islamic antiquities at the Yemen National Museum.
See item no. 112.

Ancient capitals from Aden.
See item no. 114.

Southern Arabia.
See item no. 118.

An archaeological journey to Yemen.
See item no. 119.

Archaeology in the Aden Protectorates.
See item no. 122.

A bust of a south Arabian winged goddess with nimbus in the possession of Miss Leila Ingrams.
See item no. 126.

Sculptures and inscriptions from Shabwa.
See item no. 145.

North Yemen: images of the built environment.
See item no. 355.

Three medieval mosques in the Yemen.
See item no. 359.

Two early mosques in the Yemen: a preliminary report.
See item no. 360.

Architecture of the Islamic world; its history and social meaning.
See item no. 361.

Cultural policy in the Yemen Arab Republic.
See item no. 367.

The National Museum, Ṣan'ā', YAR.
See item no. 379.

Corpus des inscriptions et antiquités sud-arabes: bibliographie générale systématique. (A collection of writings about South Arabian inscriptions and antiquities: a general systematic bibliography).
See item no. 398.

The Near East (South-west Asia and North Africa): a bibliographic study.
See item no. 401.

Folklore

377 **Folklore and folk literature in Oman and Socotra.**
T. M. Johnstone. *Arabian Studies*, vol. 1 (1974), p. 7-23.

A study of the beliefs and popular culture of the Mehris and others of Oman and of the people of the island of Socotra.

378 **Folk-remedies from Ḥaḍramawt.**
R. B. Serjeant. *Bulletin of the School of Oriental and African Studies,* vol. 18, no. 1 (1956), p. 5-8.

A translation of a Ḥaḍrami document on folk-remedies. It is in the main an itemized account of the medicinal properties of plants.

Arabian Studies.
See item no. 17.

The quarters of Tarīm and their tanṣūrahs.
See item no. 263.

Museums and Archives

379 **The National Museum, San'a', YAR.**
Salma al-Radi. *The Arab Cultural Scene* (1982), p. 132-33.

A brief note on the Ṣan'ā' National Museum.

The pre-Islamic antiquities at the Yemen National Museum.
See item no. 112.

Documents on the history of southwest Arabia: tribal warfare and foreign policy in Yemen, Aden and adjacent tribal kingdoms, 1920-29.
See item no. 219.

A Judeo-Arab house-deed from Habbān (with notes of the former Jewish communities of the Wāḥidī Sultanate).
See item no. 231.

Cultural policy in the Yemen Arab Republic.
See item no. 367.

A guide to manuscripts and documents in the British Isles relating to the Middle East and North Africa.
See item no. 391.

Mass Media

380 **Broadcasting in the Arab world.**
Douglas A. Boyd. Philadelphia: Temple University Press, 1982. 306p. map. bibliog.

A survey of radio and television in the whole of the Middle East. Pages 97-103 are relevant here for they cover North Yemen (p. 98-99) and South Yemen p. 99-102.

381 **The Arab press: news media and political process in the Arab world.**
William A. Pugh. London: Croom Helm, 1979. 250p.

A general study of the press of the Arab world. See in particular the sections on North Yemen and South Yemen.

The Middle East: a political and economic survey.
See item no. 11.

Who's who in the Arab world.
See item no. 23.

Yémen. (The Yemen).
See item no. 43.

The Arabian Peninsula: society and politics.
See item no. 252.

Cultural policy in the Yemen Arab Republic.
See item no. 367.

Education and the press in South Arabia.
See item no. 369.

A book world directory of the Arab countries, Turkey and Iran.
See item no. 384.

Directories

382 **The Middle East: a Handbook.**
Edited by Michael Adams. London: Anthony Blond, 1971. 598p. 17 maps.

A general reference handbook on the Middle East. Of particular interest are the chapters on the Republic of South Yemen (p. 263-270); and on the Yemen Arab Republic (p. 335-341). The work also includes maps of South Yemen (p. 264) and of Yemen (p. 336).

383 **Aden and South Arabia.**
Central Office of Information. London: British Information Services, 1965. 32p. 2 maps. bibliog.

A general reference work and guide to Aden and South Arabia.

384 **A book world directory of the Arab countries, Turkey and Iran.**
Compiled by Anthony Rudkin, Irene Butcher. London: Mansell; Detroit, Michigan: Gale, 1981. 143p.

The directory first lists the libraries, booksellers, publishers, newpapers and periodicals country by country. The Yemen Arab Republic occupies p. 112, and the People's Democratic Republic of Yemen p. 113. There are 13 appendixes on various library, bookselling, newspaper and periodical subjects.

The Middle East and North Africa 1981-82.
See item no. 13.

Bibliographies

385 **Arabic and Turkish source materials for the early history of Ottoman Yemen, 945/1538-976/1568.**
J. R. Blackburn. In: *Studies in the history of Arabia, vol. 1, part 2, Sources for the history of Arabia.* Riyadh. Riyadh University Press, 1979. p. 197-210.

A bibliographical study of the major sources for the Ottoman period of Yemeni history in the 16th century.

386 **Middle East and Islam: a bibliographic introduction.**
Revised and enlarged edition edited by Diana Grimwood-Jones. Zug, Switzerland: Inter Documentation Company, 1979. 429p. (Bibliotheca Asiatica, no. 15.)

A basic bibliography of Middle Eastern and Islamic studies. See in particular: 4, 'Regional bibliographies, Arabia' by G. R. Smith; also p. 168 (anthropology) and p. 215 (official publications).

387 **The Developing Areas: a classed bibliography of the Joint Bank-Fund Library, World Bank Group & International Monetary Fund, Washington, DC. 3 vols. Vol. 2. Africa and the Middle East.**
Joint Bank-Fund Library. Boston, Massachusetts: G. K. Hall, 1976. 646p.

A shelf list of some forty per cent of the holdings of the Joint Bank-Fund Library. The Yemen Arab Republic is covered on p. 642 and the People's Democratic Republic of Yemen on p. 644.

388 **Islamic Near East and North Africa: an annotated guide to books in English for non-specialists.**
David W. Littlefield. Littleton, Colorado: Libraries Unlimited, 1977. 332p.

Chapter XVI covers general works on the Arabian Peninsula (p. 176) and works on Yemen (p. 183).

389 **Bibliography on Yemen and notes on Mocha.**
Eric Macro. Coral Gables, Florida. University of Miami Press, 1960. 63p.

A useful, though now out-of-date bibliography, without a subject division. The 894 entries include general works on Arabia and works in all the major European languages as well as Arabic. The notes on Mocha concern, in the main, early European activities in the port.

390 **The Yemen: some recent literature.**
Eric Macro. *Royal Central Asian Journal*, vol. 45, no. 1 (Jan. 1958), p. 43-51.

A bibliographical survey of European literature on the Yemen.

391 **A guide to manuscripts and documents in the British Isles relating to the Middle East and North Africa.**
Compiled by Noel Matthews, M. Doreen Wainwright, edited by J. D. Pearson. Oxford: Oxford University Press, 1980. 482p.

A comprehensive guide to the documents relating to the Middle East which can be found in the United Kingdom. Readers interested in Southwest Arabia should consult the index under such headings as: 'Aden', 'Sanaa'a' (Ṣan'ā') and Yemen etc.

392 **The status of the Arab woman: a select bibliography.**
Samira Rafidi Meghdessian, under the auspices of the Institute for Women's Studies in the Arab World, Beirut University College. London: Mansell, 1980. 158p.

A bibliography of works concerning attitudes towards women in the family and in society. There are chapters covering the cultural, social, Islamic, and legal background and there is a specific chapter on Yemen (p. 157-8).

393 **A select bibliography of Yemen Arab Republic and People's Democratic Republic of Yemen.**
Simoné L. Mondésir. Durham, England: Centre for Middle Eastern and Islamic Studies, 1977. (Occasional Papers Series, no. 5)

This bibliography is divided as follows: 'General bibliographical works'; 'General reference works on Arabian Peninsula'; 'YAR-Archaeology and early history, general, historical and travel, revolution and republic, people and society and general economic conditions'; 'PDRY (with same headings), also the end of colonial rule'.

394 **Arab education 1956-1978: a bibliography.**
Veronica S. Pantelidis. London: Mansell, 1982. 552p. bibliog.

A bibliography of Arab education country by country. The People's Democratic Republic of Yemen is dealt with on p. 466-73 and the Yemen Arab Republic on p. 473-81.

395 **Index Islamicus.**
Compiled by J. D. Pearson. Cambridge, England: Heffer, 1958 (1906-55), 897p., 1962 (supplement 1956-60), 316p., 1967 (2nd supplement 1961-65), 342p.; Compiled by J. D. Pearson, Ann Walsh. London: Mansell, 1972 (3rd supplement 1966-70), 384p.; Compiled by J. D. Pearson. London: Mansell, 1977 (4th supplement 1971-75), 429p., 1983 (1976-80, part 1, articles), 539p.; Compiled by J. D. Pearson, Wolfgang Behn. London: Mansell, 1983 (1976-80, part 2, monographs), 348p.

A bibliography of articles, on all aspects of Islamic studies, published in periodicals, Festschriften, conference reports and other collective works.

396 **The Quarterly Index Islamicus: Current Books, Articles and Papers on Islamic Studies.**
Edited by J. D. Pearson. London: Mansell, Jan. 1977-April 1982. quarterly. Compiled by J. D. Pearson, W. A. Lockwood, G. J. Roper. London: Mansell, July 1982- . quarterly.

Lists current books and articles from a wide range of periodicals. The entries are arranged by country.

397 **The modern Arab woman: a bibliography.**
Michelle Raccagni. Metuchen, New Jersey; London: Scarecrow Press, 1978. 237p.

This bibliography covers works on the social and legal position of Arab women in general but with particular reference to Egypt and Tunisia. Chapter XIV is on South Yemen and Chapter XIX concerns the Yemen Arab Republic.

398 **Corpus des inscriptions et antiquités sud-arabes: bibliographie générale systématique.** (A collection of writings about South Arabian inscriptions and antiquities: a general systematic bibliography).
Christian Robin. Louvain, Belgium: Edition Peeters, 1977. 428p.

A bibliography of the pre-Islamic South Arabian civilizations, and much more besides! The items are listed under the following heading: 'General Works'; 'Language and Script'; 'Non-South Arabian Epigraphic and Literary Sources'; 'Epigraphy'; 'Art and Archaeology'; 'Religions'; 'Historical ancilliaries'; 'History'; 'The Natural Environment of South Arabia'; and 'Allied Cultures'. The work also contains (p. 340-76) a bibliography of travel and exploration in South Arabia which must be as near as possible to comprehensive. Bibliographic entries under each subject heading are arranged chronologically.

399 **American doctoral dissertations on the Arab world, 1883-1974.**
Compiled by George Dimitri Selim. Washington, DC: Library of Congress, 1976. 173p.

A comprehensive bibliography of all doctoral theses accepted by universities in the United States and Canada. The bibliography is in alphabetical order by author's name.

400 **Theses on Islam, the Middle East and North-west Africa 1880-1978.**
Peter Sluglett. London: Mansell, 1983. 147p.

A comprehensive bibliography of all higher degree theses accepted by universities in the United Kingdom and Ireland. A section on the Yemen is to be found on p. 112-14, with sub-titles: 'Agriculture'; 'Economics'; 'Geography'; 'Geology'; 'History'; 'Language and literature'; 'Law'; and 'Social studies'.

401 **The Near East (South-west Asia and North Africa): a bibliographic study.**
Compiled by Jalal Zuwiyya. Metuchen, New Jersey: Scarecrow Press, 1973. 392p.

A bibliography of the Arab world, plus Iran, Israel and Turkey. Part 1 is divided by subject: 'Reference works'; 'Art and archaeology'; 'Economic structure'; 'Education'; 'Geography'; 'History'; 'Language and literature'; 'Law'; 'Performing arts'; 'Philosophy'; 'Political structures'; 'Science'; and 'Social organisations'. Part 2 has a country by country division, Yemen occupying p. 306-409.

The Middle East and North Africa 1981-82.
See item no. 13.

Yemen Arab Republic.
See item no. 346.

Index

The index is a single alphabetical sequence of authors (personal and corporate), titles of publications and subjects. Index entries refer both to the main items and to other works mentioned in the notes to each item. Title entries are in italics. Numeration refers to the items as numbered.

C

Diaries
coffee agent in 18th-century Mocha 165
Leigh, John Studdy 207
Diem, W. 234
Diplomacy, US 318
Directories 13, 382-384
Diseases 4
Dissertations
United Kingdom and Ireland – bibliograaphy 400
United States – bibliography 399
District names 36
Doctor among the bedouins 251
Documents on the history of southwest Arabia: tribal warfare and foreign policy in Yemen, Aden and adjacent tribal Kingdoms, 1920-29 219
Doe, B. 114-118, 207, 357
Donovan, M. 335
Donzel, E. van 134, 136, 178
Dostal, W. 1, 248
Durham University
Trevelyan College 355
Dutch 48, 319
Dynasties
Ayyubids 161, 167, 169, 176-177, 179
Fatimids 302
Islamic 130
Isma'īlī 175
Mutawakkilite 193, 302
pre-Islamic 149
Qāsimī 302
Rasulids 130, 170, 176-177, 302
Sharaf al-Dīn 302
Yemeni, territorial boundaries 38
Zaydīs 130, 160, 298, 302

E

Earthquakes 28
East india Company 165, 222
East is West 95
Eastern Aden Protectorate 290, 305
geology 29
'Ingrams' Peace' 286, 306
politics 285
Economic conditions 271
bibliography 393, 400
Ḥujariyyah 267
Jews 230
tribal autonomy in Banū Ḥushaysh 248
Economic development 11, 24, 44, 47, 173, 275, 280, 282, 295, 303, 324, 326, 328-332, 334, 349
Economy 6, 11, 13-16, 20, 23, 43-44, 47, 275, 322-333, 337, 372
bibliographies 346, 387, 393, 400-401
impact of brain drain 352
planning 323
prospects for the 1980s 333
South Arabia 280
statistics 328-329, 354
technology transfer 374
Education 6, 11, 23-24, 43, 252, 260, 303, 323, 329, 337, 370, 372
Aden in the 19th century 7
Aden in the 1940s 8
Algeria 370
bibliographies 394, 401
culture 367
Egypt 370
family planning 225
Ḥaḍramawt 368
Iraq 370
Islamic 370
job opportunities for school and university leavers 351
Jordan 370
Kuwait 370
Lebanon 370
Libya 370
Morocco 370
Palestine 370
post-secondary 369
Saudi Arabia 370
South Arabia 252, 369
statistics 354
Sudan 370
Syria 370
teacher training 369
technical 369
Tunisia 370
Egypt
Ayyubids 176
education 370
expedition of Carsten Niebuhr 66, 83
policy toward the Yemen in the 1960s 198
revolutionary change in 1950s 304
revolutions and military rule 281
women – bibliography 397

G

H

J

K

L

Leigh, John Studdy
diary 207
Levant
trade 338-339
Leveson Gower, W. 77
Lévi-Provençal, E. 168
Levine, E. 299
Lewcock, R. 1, 18, 359-361
Lewis, B. 134, 136, 178
Lewis, D. B. 326-327
Libraries 384
'l-Haqq, al-Hādī ilā 160
Libya
education 370
revolutions and military rule 281
Life and customs 4, 9, 12, 47, 239, 261, 299
18th century 83
19th century 79, 104
Aden 7-8
bibliography 393
Ḥaḍramawt 86, 178, 254
Mehris 377
Socotra 56, 58
South Arabian 148, 239
Literature 17
bibliographies 400-401
colloquial South Arabian 239
folk literature in Oman and Socotra 377
ibex hunt 265
Ḥajjah prisons 375
Little, T. 211
Littlefield, D. W. 388
Locknat, J. 351
Lockwood, W. 18
Lockwood, W. A. 396
Löfgren, O. 168
Lowick, N. 18
al-Luḥayyah
18-century account 66
Luqman, F. M. 44-45
Lunt, J. 75

M

McClintock, D. W. 313-314
McFarlane, J. 66
McFarlane, K. 66
McGrath, R. 63
McKee, D. 61
McLean, N. 76
McMullen, C. J. 318
Macro, E. 77, 212, 319, 389-390
Maḥram Bilqîs *see* Mārib.
Ma'īn
pre-Islamic monarchic institutions 156
Major companies of the Arab world 336
Makhlouf, C. 257
Maktari, A. M. A. 1, 345
Malyneux, M. D. 258
Mammals
'Abd-al-Kūri 105
Middle East 106
Socotra 105
Mammals of Arabia 106
Ma'n gypsies 262
Manākhah
social inequality 249
Manpower requirements 225, 327
brain drain and problems of manpower training 352
job opportunities for school and university leavers 351
scientific 373
Mansfield, P. 11
Mansur, A. 78
Manufacturing industry 329
Manzoni, R. 79
Maps and atlases 27, 33, 35-37, 49, 63, 382
16th century 49
Aden's defences 131
administrative divisions 34
bibliography 346
cartographic surveys 227
distribution of mammals in the Middle East 106
Ḥaḍramawt 30
Islamic history 38
land use 33, 34
Niebuhr, Carsten 39
north-west Yemen 40
population distribution 34
Socotra 57-58, 127
Southern Arabia 41-42
Maréchaux, P. 12
Mārib 54, 65
archaeological report 113, 125, 153
dam 125
inscriptions 149
Market consultancy report to the Land Resources Division, Ministry of Overseas Development, on the

N

Q

R

S

T

Y

Z

Map of The Yemens

This map shows the more important towns and other features.

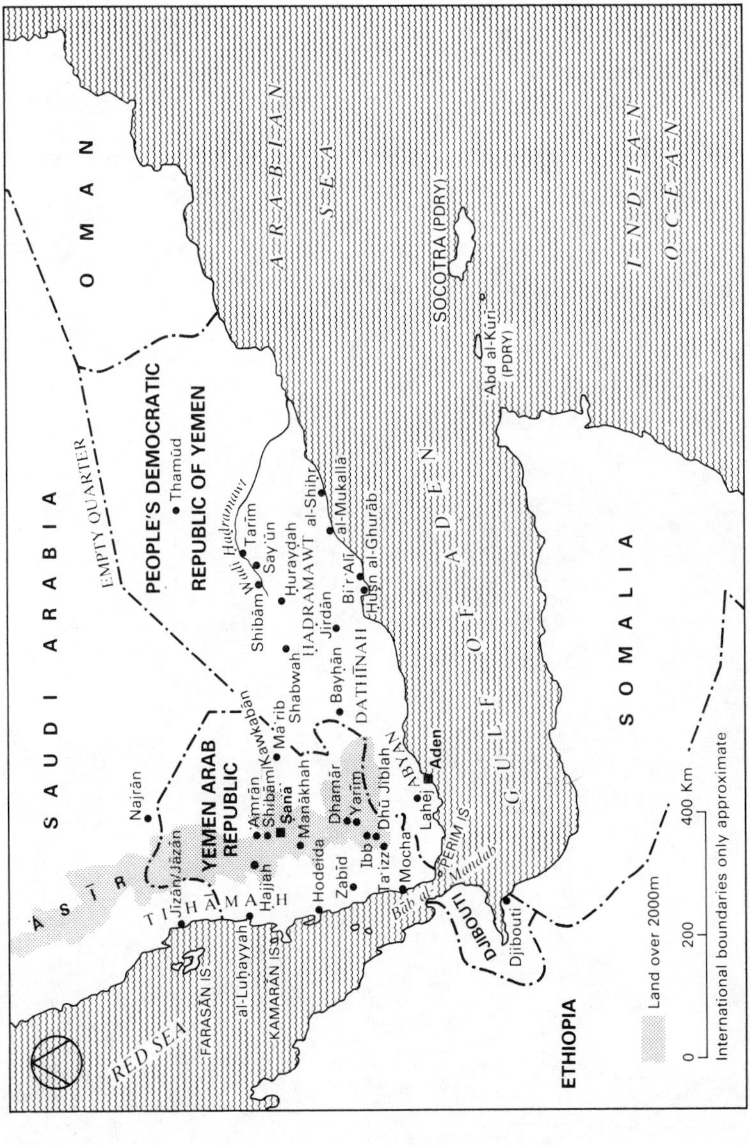